More Painting Birds in Gouache

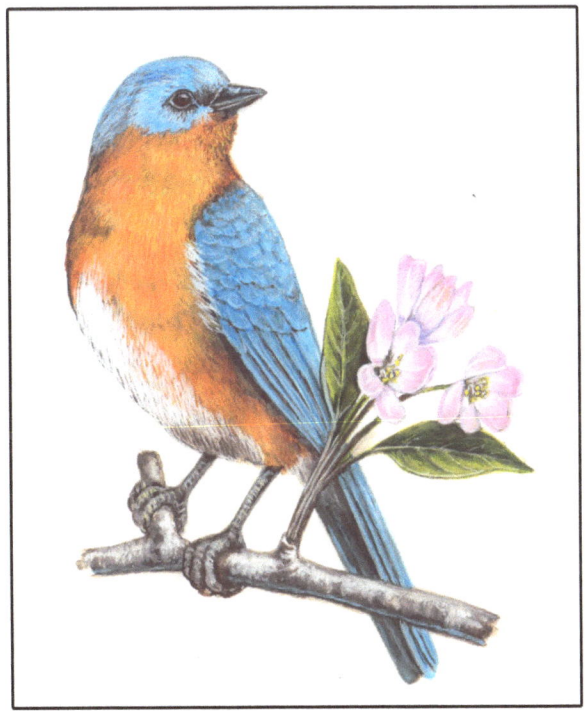

Written and Illustrated
by
Sandy Williams

© Sandra L. Williams 2016

Index

More Painting Birds in Gouache

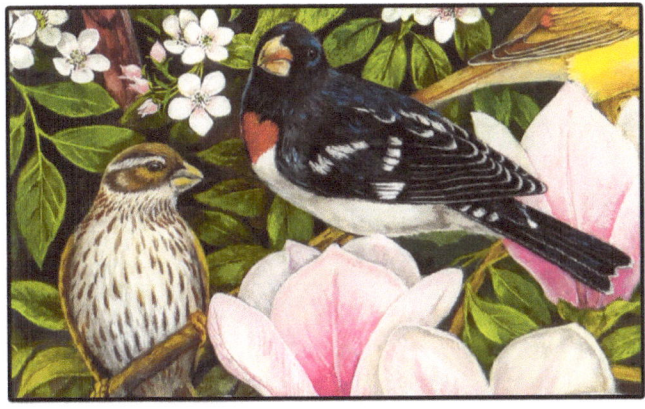

Introduction

Birds are one of the great wonders of the natural world, most of them living in three dimensions while we humans are confined to two. They've been depicted in our art work for centuries and our paintings and sculptures of them have reflected the materials and sensibilities of the various time periods. We now have a plethora of different media to work with and I've found gouache to be one of the best and easiest to work with to show all those little details in the feathers and shiny eyes.

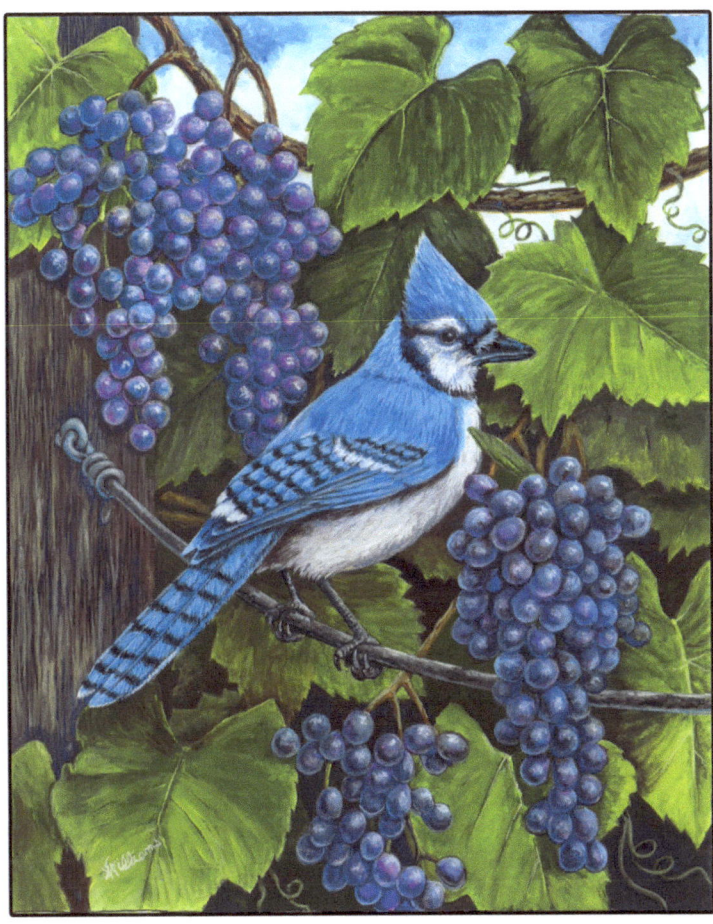

This series of workbooks is meant to be a stepping stone. I can show you one way to do something but enjoy experimenting to see what works for you -- what most helps you create the piece of art you're aiming for!

"Blue Jay & Grapes"
8" x 10", gouache

Gouache

(pronounced gwash)

I've tried many mediums to paint my detailed illustrations but I always come back to gouache, an opaque watercolor. Oils are beautiful and lush but painting in oils involves using chemicals that often have strong odors and the slow drying time can be a problem. Acrylics are fast drying but once dry they can't be reworked. Personally, I have a problem controlling transparent watercolor and it's very challenging for me. But gouache, with its colors that can be either brilliant or subtle, can be layered on and reworked even after its been dry for lengthy periods of time. Blending can make subtle variations in color and value and, along with precise detail, can bring your subject to life. Gouache is economical because, even after the dabs of paint have dried on your palette, they can be reconstituted with water so there's little waste. Because we often work with thick layers of gouache and sometimes use a "dry brush" technique gouache can be hard on brushes. Mine wear out quickly so I don't buy the most expensive ones -- just be sure you have the tiniest ones that can make a fine point. One of the great advantages of gouache is that it's very "forgiving." If you find that a certain area is not working just paint over it and start again.

Please note: It's easy to get lost in painting a detailed illustration, all bent over your work. But it's not good for the human body to sit in one place for long periods of time. Take frequent breaks -- get up and stretch, look at your work from a different angle. Also, don't forget, some of the pigments in many paints are toxic so don't point up your brush by putting the tip in your mouth.

Start by squeezing out spots of paint about this size

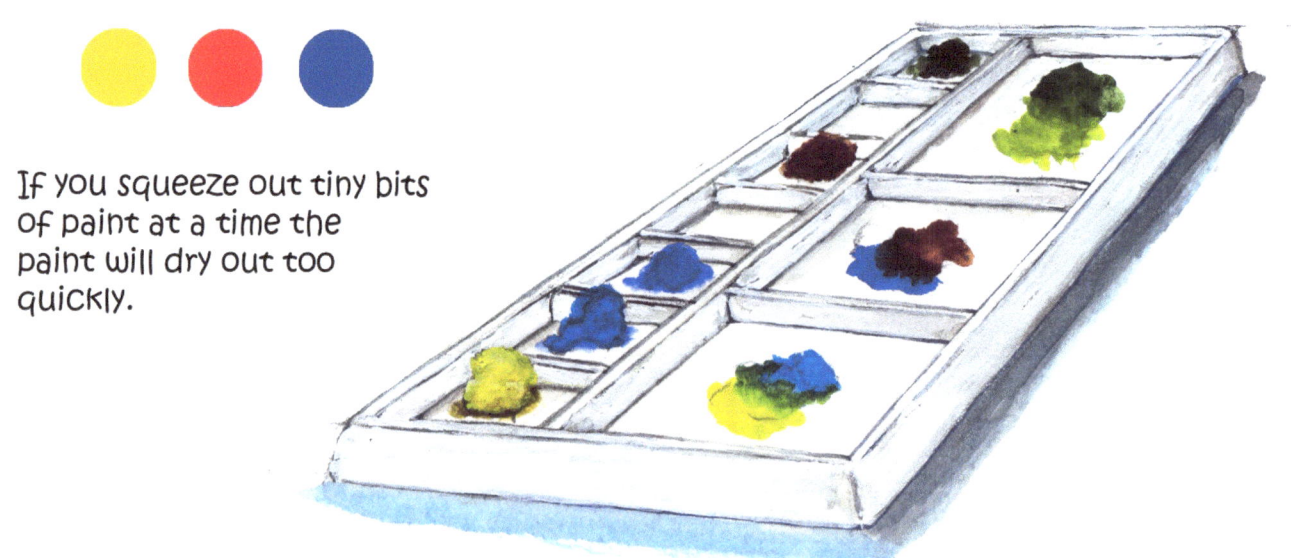

If you squeeze out tiny bits of paint at a time the paint will dry out too quickly.

2

More Painting Birds in Gouache
Materials List

PENCILS -- I generally use a softer pencil, like a 4B, to draw with but use whatever you're comfortable with. Just make sure that you don't make your marks so hard that they're hard to erase. I use a kneaded eraser because it won't leave little crumbly bits of material that have to be brushed off.

PAPER -- I recommend using hot press watercolor paper, preferably 140 #, although a little lighter weight would be OK, too. Some artists use illustration board, vellum or bristol. I use Arches 140# hot press because it has a nice, smooth surface to make detailing easier and crisper looking. Experiment and try some different papers. One half standard size sheet should be plenty for this course.

PALETTE -- It should be white so you can see exactly what color you're mixing. If you don't have a palette a white paper plate works fine. It's just a little harder to transport wet paint if you have to move around.

WATER CONTAINER -- Use whatever you have on hand. At home I use thoroughly cleaned plastic cat food containers-- no breakage problem.

TRANSFER PAPER -- Depending on how you transfer your images you may or may not need some plain tracing paper. An 11" x 14" sheet folded in half should do. Cover one side completely with soft graphite. To transfer your image, first put your paper down on a firm surface. Put your graphite paper, graphite side down, on top of that. Then put the drawing you want to transfer on top of that. Tape securely. Using a hard pencil or stylus, trace over your lines. From time to time check to see that your lines are transferring correctly. Or use a light box if you have one available, or even a sunny window.

BRUSHES -- You'll probably need three small watercolor brushes: a 4/0 small round, a #1 small round and, if you can find one, a 20/0 round.

GOUACHE -- The ten tubes listed here will give you enough variety of colors to complete all the illustrations in this course. The brand I use is Winsor & Newton but that's not a requirement.

Permanent White	Opera Pink
Olive Green	Primary Blue
Burnt Umber	Ultramarine Blue
Burnt Sienna	Marigold Yellow
Spectrum Yellow	Spectrum Red

How to Use this Workbook

As you go through this workbook you'll notice that the steps for painting a leaf, for example, are split up over many pages that also contain steps for painting the bird or petals or grass. I organized the workbook this way to get as much information in as few pages as possible but I don't necessarily work that way. I generally fully complete the background elements first -- the flowers, branches, grass or sky -- before I begin to finish the bird. So, if you'd like, feel free to follow the thread through the steps for one element and then go back and pick up another one.

Just remember, the things that are in the background are generally painted first so that you don't have to repaint the edges of the elements in front.

If you'd like to add a bit of sky or far off trees or other elements, let your creativity flow. But paint the background first, planning ahead so that your lights and darks don't interfere with those of the bird and effect the readability.

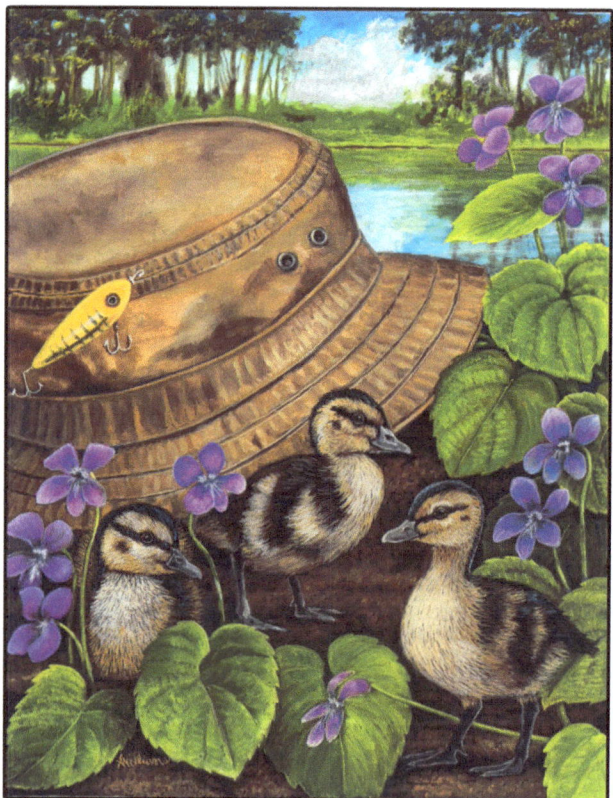

"Ducklings &
Old Fishing Hat"
8"x10", gouache

1

Color and Value

Color

Don't worry if your colors don't match those in this demonstration exactly. Color is ever changing -- the color of a chipmunk may be almost red if he's sitting in the sun but more of a dull brown if he's hiding in the shadows. One thing to avoid is a flat area of an even tone of color. This will look unnatural. These demonstrations will show you how to work in layers and blend them to make beautiful and subtle variations in color to make your subject look more realistic.

Value

Value is the lightness or darkness of the color you're working with. If your painting has almost all the same values it will lose contrast and may be dull or uninteresting. Be sure to use a full range in your work. You won't be using black in these demonstrations but will instead be using a mixture of Burnt Umber and Ultramarine Blue for the darkest values. To lighten this mixture you'll add White. See the illustration below to see the full range of values you can make using this important mixture.

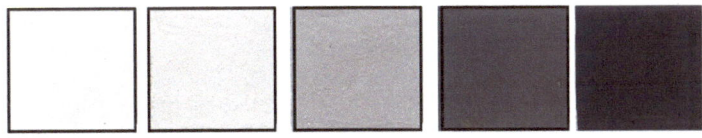

Burnt Umber/Ultramarine Blue: light to dark

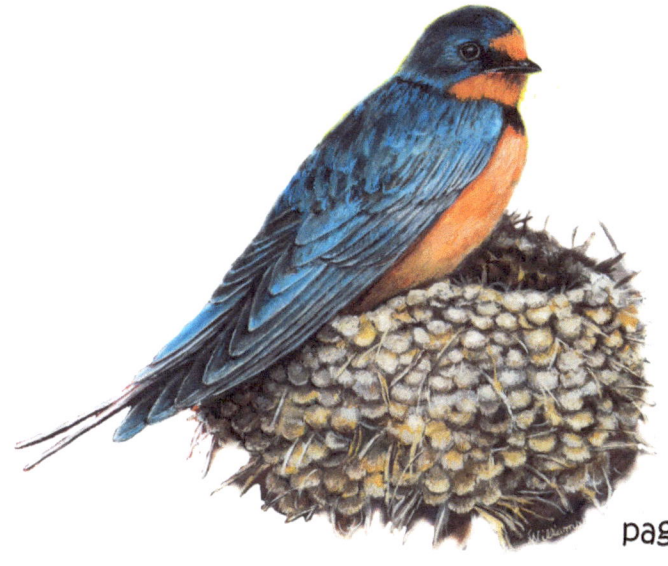

"Barn Swallow"
8" x 10", gouache

Underpainting, Blending & Watch Those Edges!

There are two very important techniques to learn when using gouache.

Underpainting -- For most of my illustrations I paint "light over dark." That means that, even though my subject may end up being white or a very light color, I still first paint it with a dark value gouache, usually a mixture of Burnt Umber and Ultramarine Blue. If I'm painting a bird it's almost like painting the shadows under all the feathers first. Then, when I start painting lighter elements over the underpainting, the strokes really pop out. If anyone happens to walk in and see my painting at this stage when I've painted my whites a dark gray they will be completely mystified and I'm sure feel sorry for me, thinking I've completely lost my touch. But almost every painting starts this way.

Blending -- If your paint strokes are left unblended and hard edged your subject will not look realistic. It's fine to leave some strokes unblended for emphasis, but blending them creates subtle variations in color and value and it will look more realistic. You want to avoid flat areas of color. By blending your layers some of the dark value from below will mix with your lighter value above when you add water. Just be careful to use a very slightly damp brush when you blend or you will copletely blend out your strokes. If that happens just repaint the darker layer, repaint your light strokes over it and reblend.

To blend, dip your brush in water and then run it over a paper towel to remove any excess. Gently move the brush parallel to your strokes to take the hard edges away. This can be time consuming but well worth it in the end.

Edges -- It's also very important to watch the outside edges of your bird, especially if you have a white background. You don't want them to look so sharp that your bird looks pasted on the page. To soften them either take a damp brush and gently blend away that hard edge or take a little white gouache and work it into the edge to lighten them.

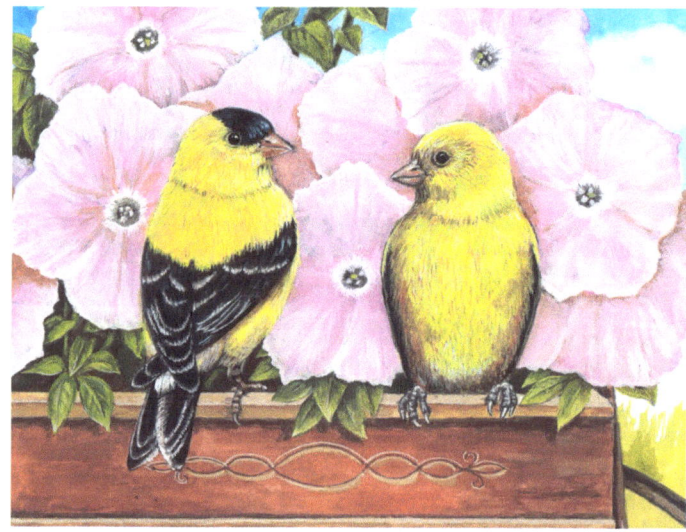

"Goldfinches &
Old Wagon"
8" x 10"
gouache

Eastern Bluebird
(Sialia sialis)

Colors Used: Permanent White, Burnt Umber, Ultramarine Blue, Olive Green, Marigold Yellow, Burnt Sienna, Opera Pink, Primary Blue, Spectrum Yellow

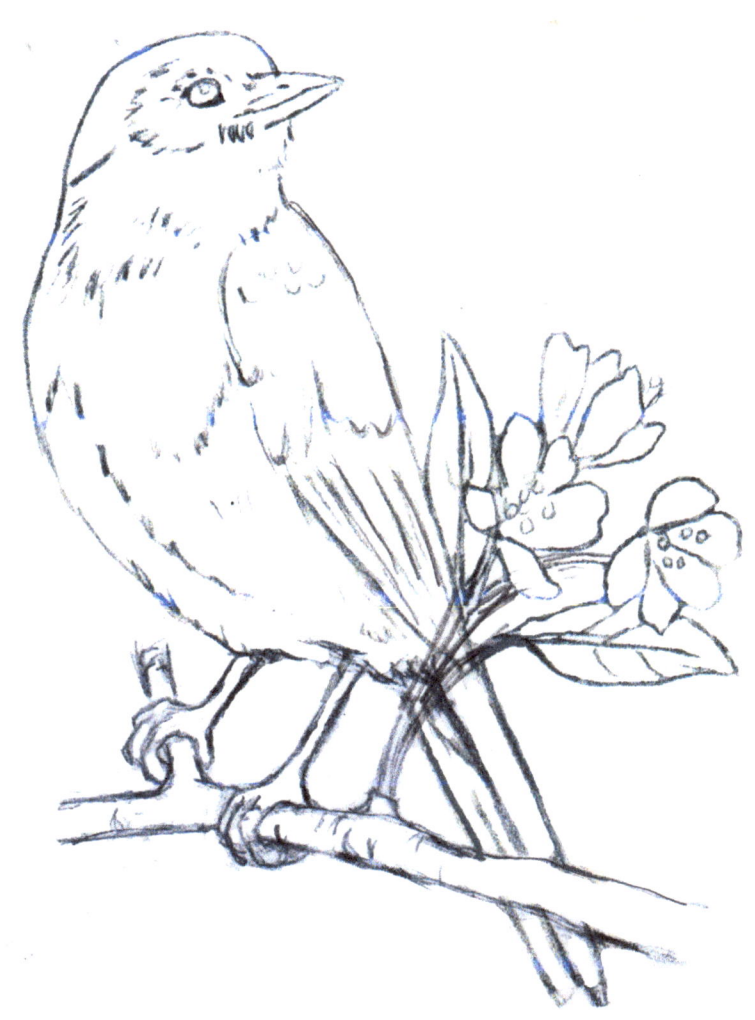

Use this sheet to transfer the image to your sheet of hot press watercolor paper or illustration board.

Eastern Bluebird

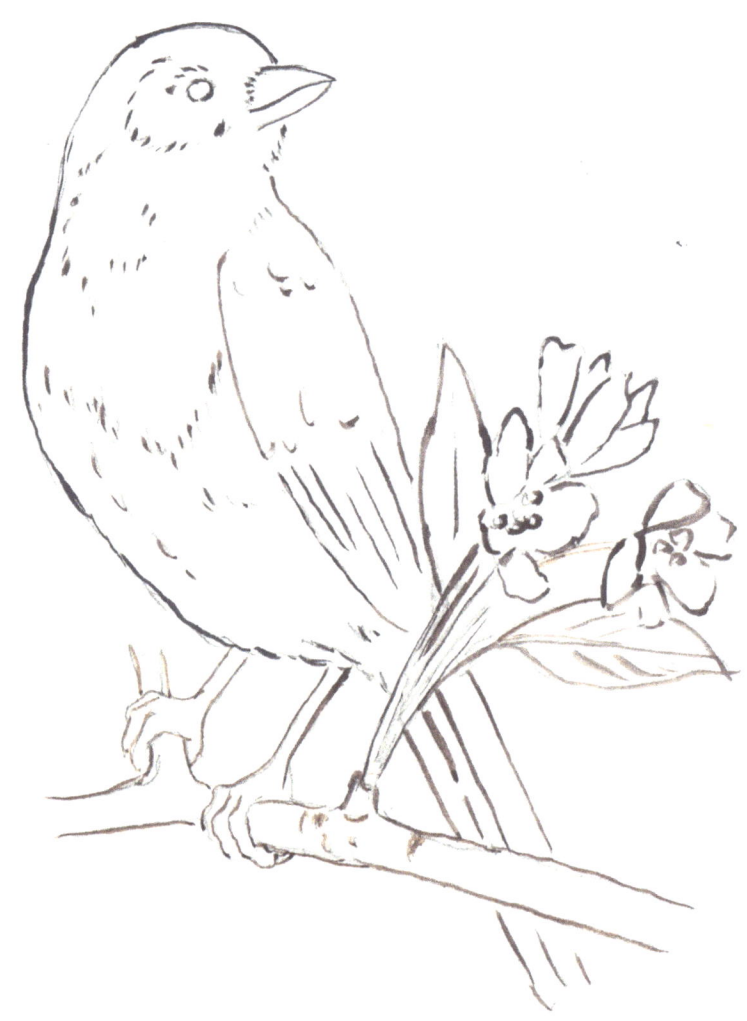

(1)

Transfer your drawing to the watercolor paper (or whatever substrate you've chosen). You'll be adding layers of gouache so the lines have to be dark enough to hold up while you're painting. I generally go over my lines with a thin, dark value of gouache made by mixing Burnt Umber and Ultramarine Blue. Keep your lines narrow. Use a thinner wash than the one you'll use for the upper layers. Use one of your smallest brushes. If your pencil lines are dark enough you may want to skip this step.

Eastern Bluebird

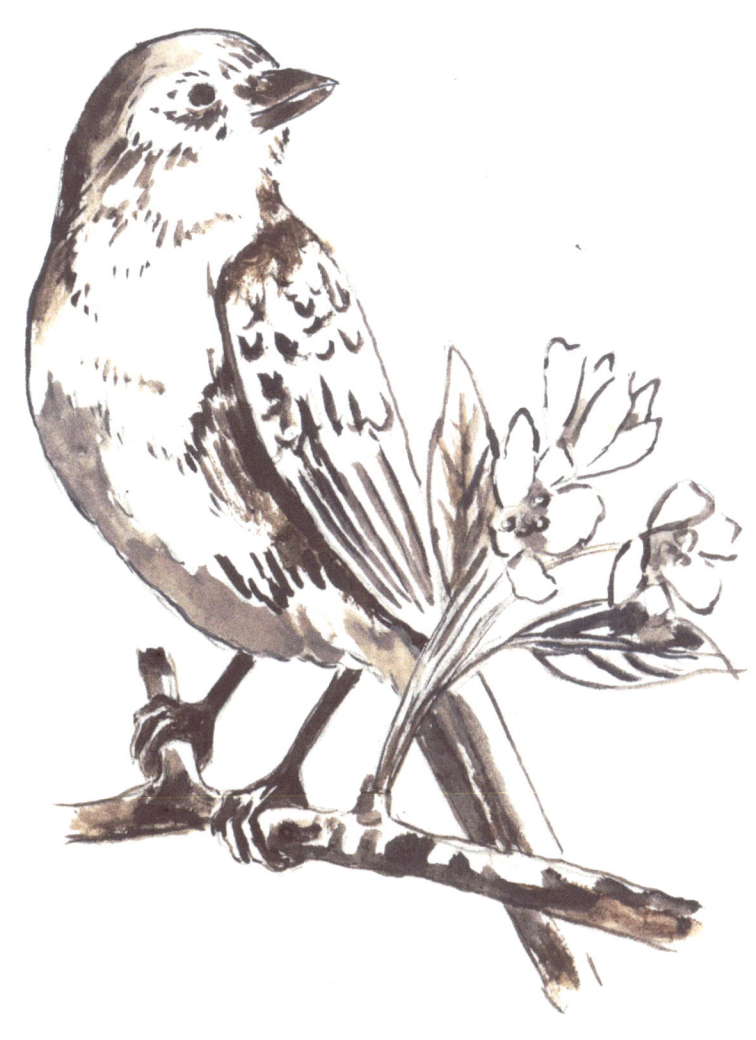

(2)

The dark value underpainting -- With a thin wash of a mixture of Burnt Umber and Ultramarine Blue, paint in the darkest places in the painting of the Bluebird. Because the colors of the Bluebird are so brilliant the underpainting won't cover the whole bird -- just where the darkest areas will be. A dark underpainting would dull the bright blue. One thing holds true. If an area is going to end up being white it's generally best to paint it a medium value gray first. So even though the belly of the Bluebird will be white, first paint it gray. When you add a thicker layer of White over it and begin to blend lovely nuances of the gray color will be created.

Eastern Bluebird

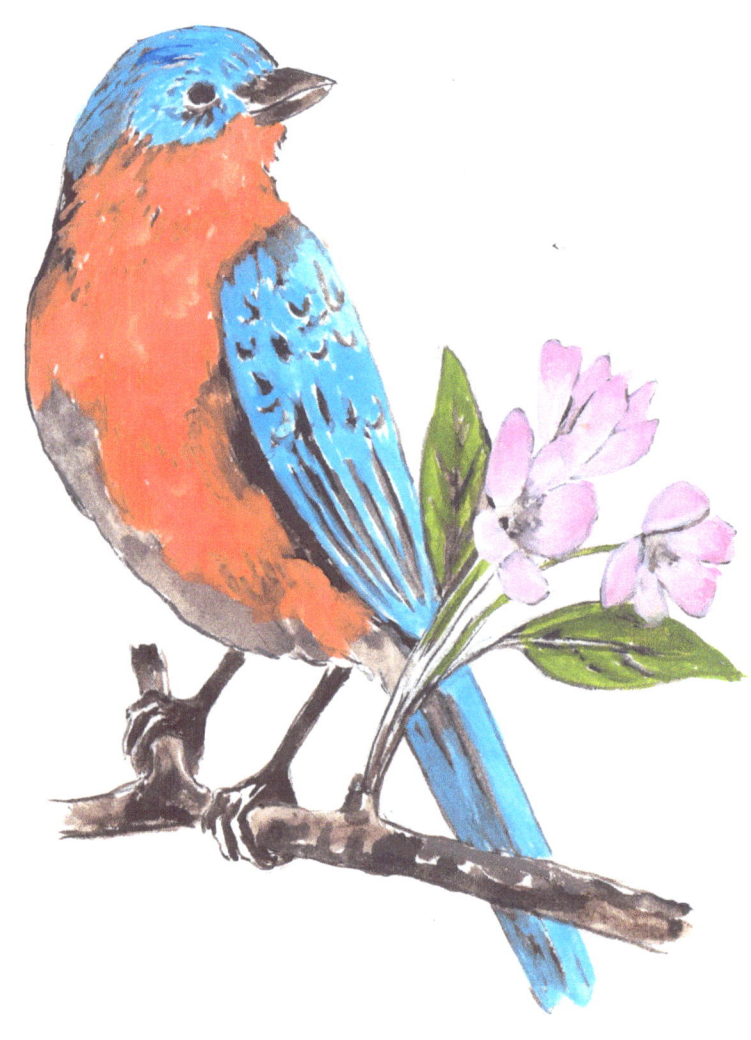

(3)

The Bird --Add White to Primary Blue and paint over the blue portions of the
Bluebird. Use Marigold Yellow to paint the neck and sides of the
breast. Marigold Yellow is a bit transparent and the lines you
painted previously will show through. Don't worry about being
too exact at this stage.
Leaves -- With a mixture of Spectrum Yellow tinted with Olive
Green paint in the two leaves.
Flower Petals -- Mix White with Opera Pink. Paint the tips of the petals
Branch -- Paint the top of the branch with a thin wash of
Burnt Umber mixed with Ultramarine Blue.

Eastern Bluebird

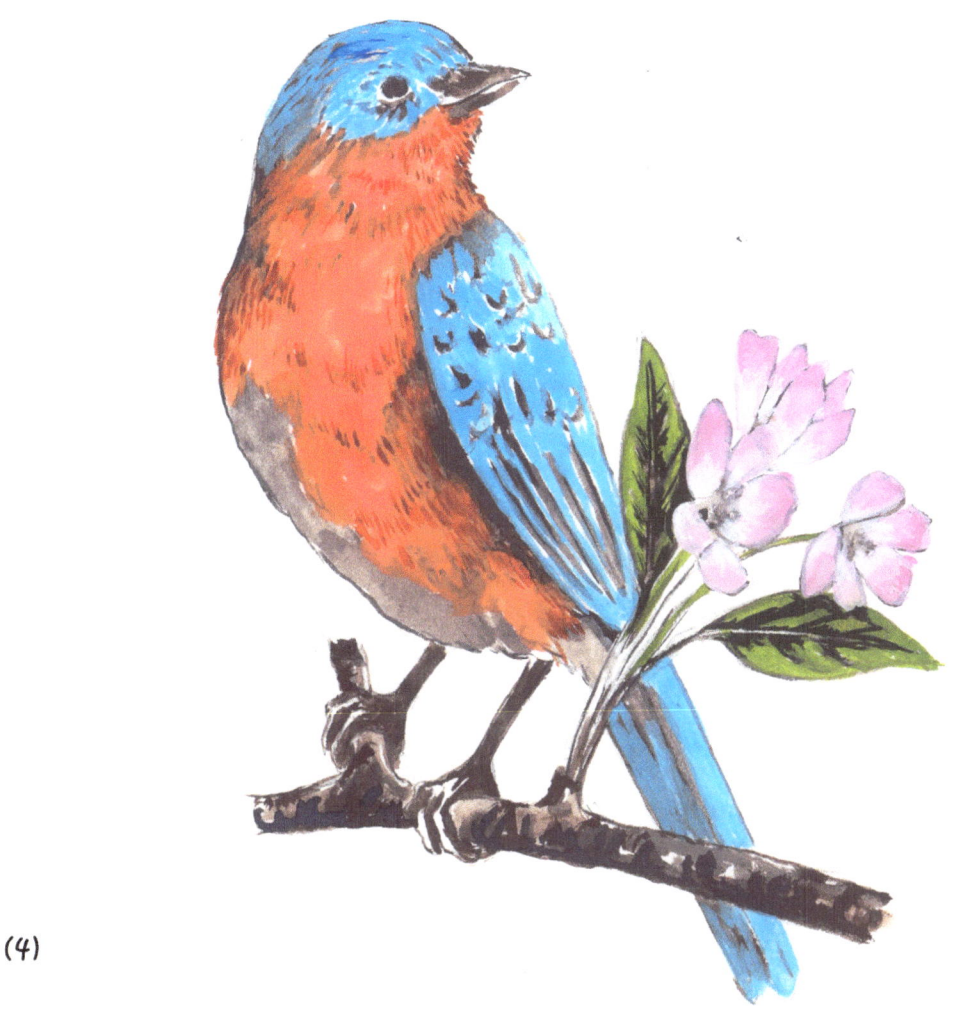

(4)

The Bird-- With Burnt Umber paint short, fine strokes in the areas you previously painted Marigold Yellow, always stroking in the direction of the feather pattern.
Leaves-- Add Ultramarine Blue to Olive Green and paint in the darkest areas of the leaves.
Petals -- With White paint the centers of the apple blossoms with strokes going fro the center to the outside edges of the petals, going about half way up.
Branch -- With your darkest value of the Burnt Umber and Ultramarine Blue mixture, make strokes curving around the contour of the branch on the lower sides. This will start to establish dimension for the branch.

Eastern Bluebird

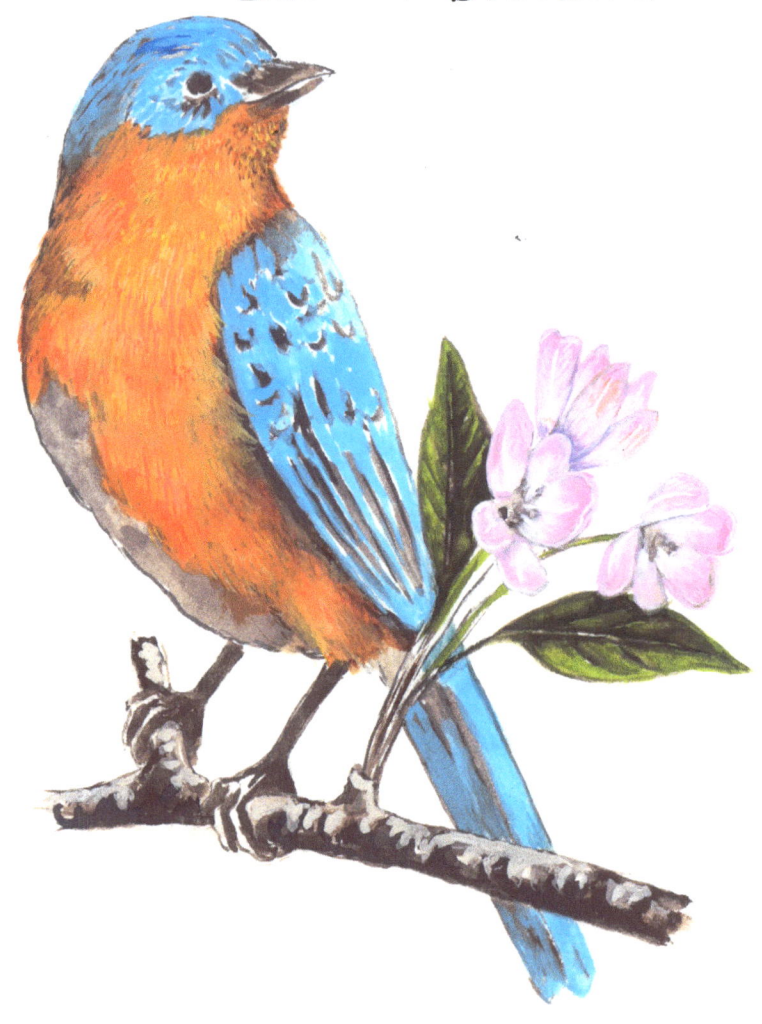

(5)

Bluebird-- At this point the orange in the breast is much too bright. With a damp brush, begin to blend the dark strokes of Burnt Umber you made previously. This is a back and forth process. You don't want to add too many dark strokes or you will lose the brightness of the feathers. When you've blended your dark strokes, add Spectrum Yellow to White and add some light strokes, also blending them in a little. What you want to avoid is a large, flat area of color. Cover this whole area with small strokes, gently blending them in. For the lightest areas add more White to the Spectrum Yellow. For the darker areas add Burnt Sienna. Keep doing this until the whole area is textured. Some strokes should show so don't blend too much.

Leaves -- With a damp brush, blend the two shades of green together. The leaves will still look too dark. Don't worry about keeping the veins even -- they'll be painted in at the end.

Petals -- With White, paint in a center vein in each petal. Blend the white from the center outward toward the edge of the petals, making a smooth transition. For the small darker ares of the petals add a little Primary Blue to your mixture. You'll probably have to add more Opera Pink mixed with White as you go along. Gently blend and soften your strokes.

Branch -- With pure White, paint along the top edge of the branch, following the contours. It will start turning darker right away because of the dark underpainting.

Eastern Bluebird

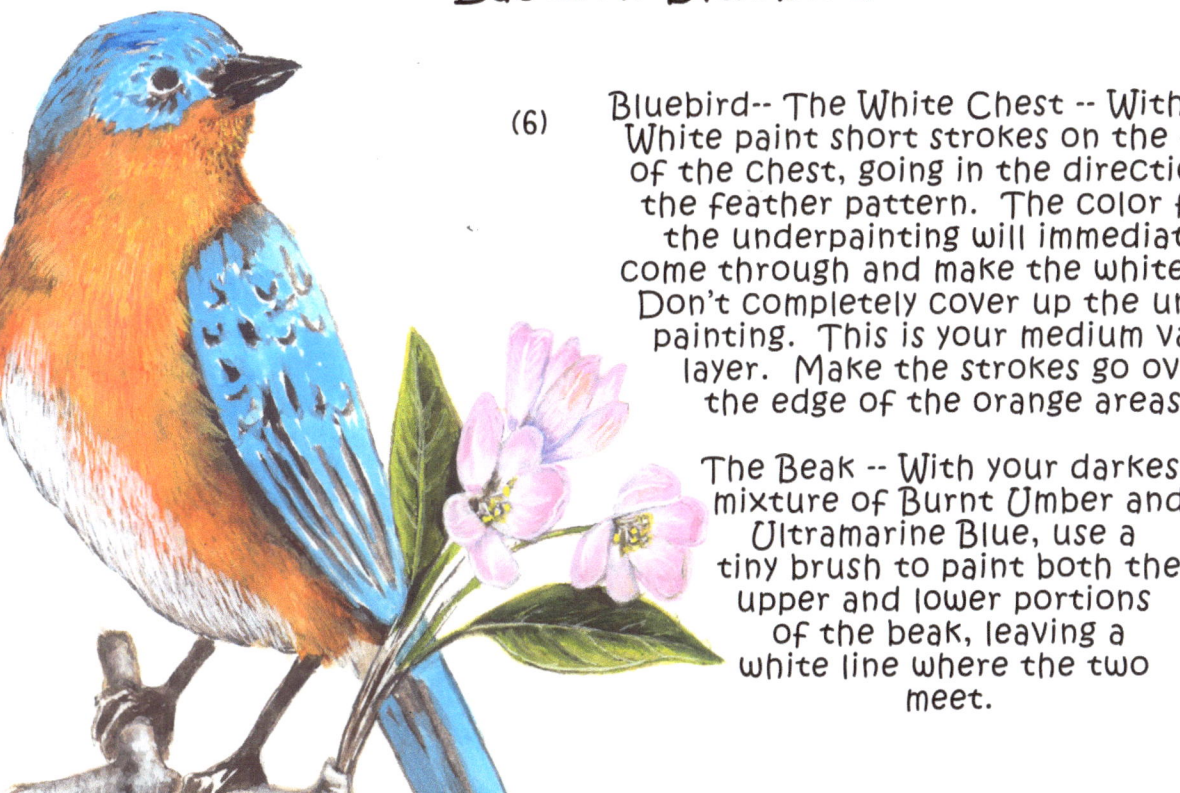

(6)

Bluebird -- The White Chest -- With pure White paint short strokes on the front of the chest, going in the direction of the feather pattern. The color from the underpainting will immediately come through and make the white gray. Don't completely cover up the under-painting. This is your medium value layer. Make the strokes go over the edge of the orange areas.

The Beak -- With your darkest mixture of Burnt Umber and Ultramarine Blue, use a tiny brush to paint both the upper and lower portions of the beak, leaving a white line where the two meet.

Leaves -- To finish detailing the leaves, mix Spectrum Yellow, White, Olive Green and just a touch of Burnt Sienna to tone it down a little. Paint a lighter value where the light hits the leaf and use more Olive Green in the mix to paint the areas that are darker. Blend. You'll probably have to add more of the light and dark values and reblend as you go along. When you have the leaves the right values, add the veins with White tinted with Spectrum Yellow. Also, paint a thin line on the front edges of the leaves to give them a 3D effect.
Apple Blossom Centers -- Use pure White to paint the filaments and Spectrum Yellow mixed with White to paint the anthers. If your strokes don't show up, add a mixture of Burnt Umber and Ultramarine Blue behind them and blend it in.
Branch --Blend the White along the top of the branch into the darker underpainting. It will turn dark very quickly so you'll have to keep adding White. As you blend you'll be creating subtle, lovely color shifts in the branch. Mix Primary Blue with White and paint reflected light along the bottom of the branch. Blend it slightly with a damp brush.

Eastern Bluebird

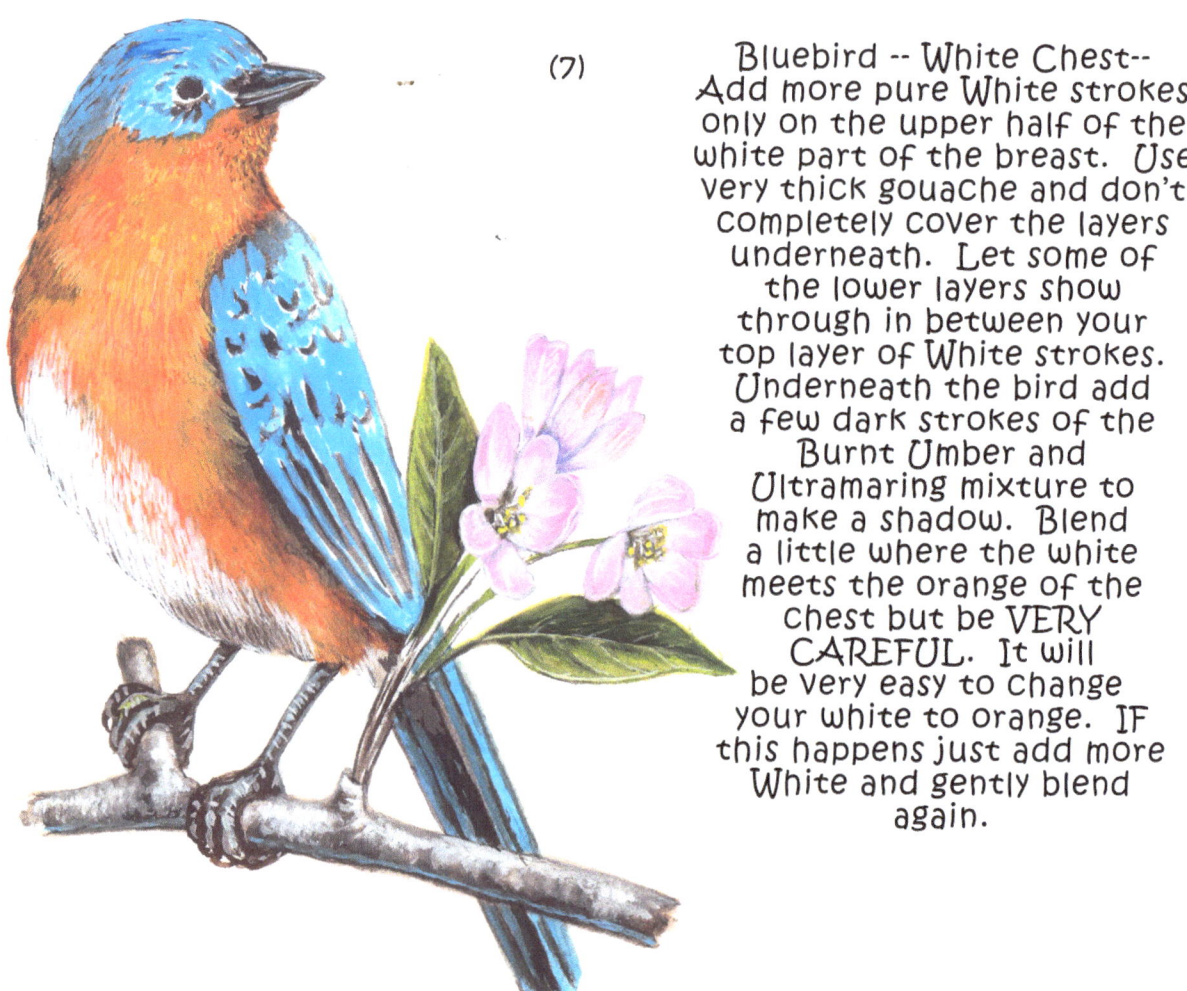

(7)

Bluebird -- White Chest-- Add more pure White strokes only on the upper half of the white part of the breast. Use very thick gouache and don't completely cover the layers underneath. Let some of the lower layers show through in between your top layer of White strokes. Underneath the bird add a few dark strokes of the Burnt Umber and Ultramaring mixture to make a shadow. Blend a little where the white meets the orange of the chest but be VERY CAREFUL. It will be very easy to change your white to orange. IF this happens just add more White and gently blend again.

The Beak -- With White, paint two very narrow lines on the edges of the upper and lower beak. Make a tiny upside down semicircle for the nostril and then use White mixed with Primary Blue to paint some reflected light on the top surface of the beak. Blend gently.

Legs & Feet -- With a dark ixture of Burnt Umber and Ultramarine Blue, shape the legs and feet. Use White to add small detail lines.

Tail -- With a dark mixture of Burnt Umber and Ultramarine Blue, paint lines running from the top of the tail to the tip. Blend off the sharp edges.

Eastern Bluebird

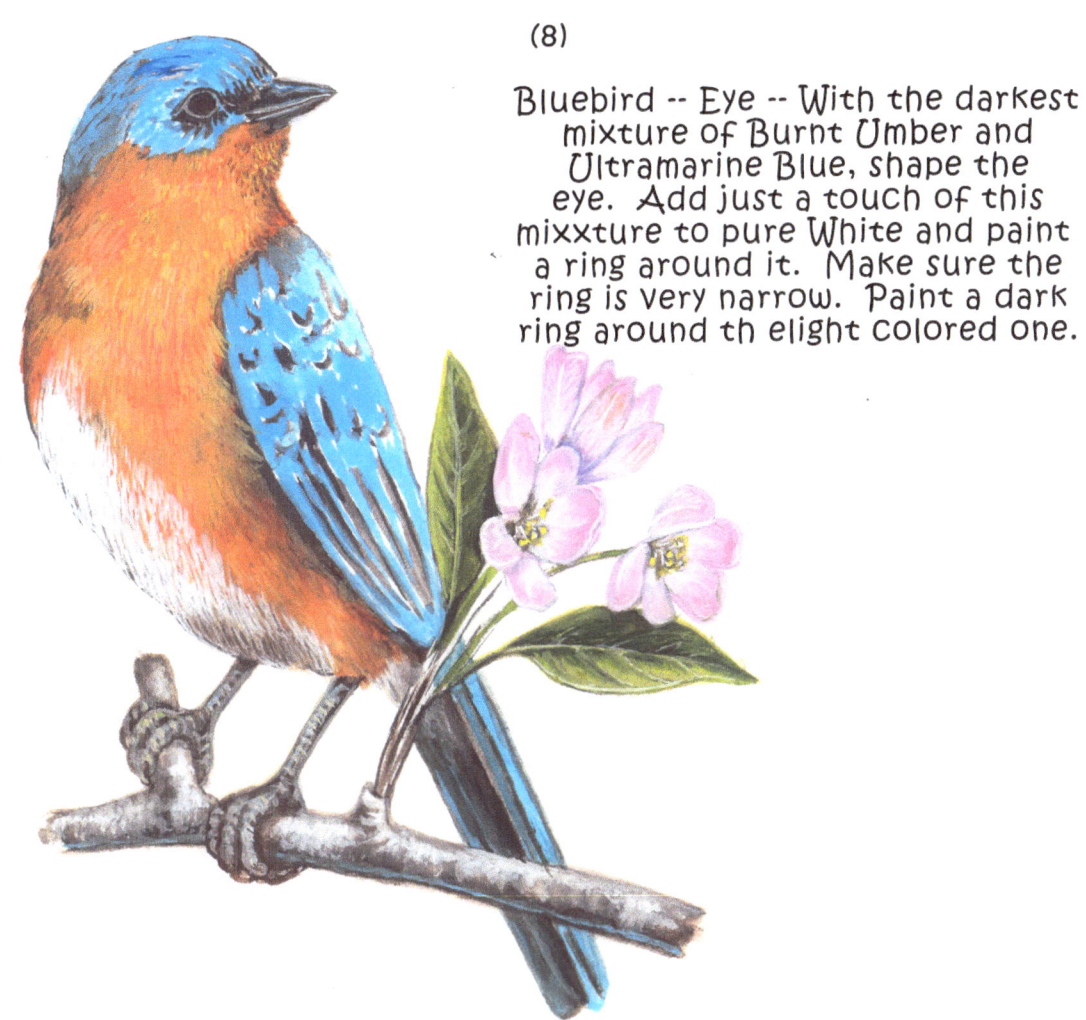

(8)

Bluebird -- Eye -- With the darkest mixture of Burnt Umber and Ultramarine Blue, shape the eye. Add just a touch of this mixxture to pure White and paint a ring around it. Make sure the ring is very narrow. Paint a dark ring around th elight colored one.

Legs & Feet -- Blend the strokes you painted previously. You'll have to add more white to the tiny semicircles that go around the legs and then probably more of your dark value of Burnt Umber and Ultramarine Blue, too. This is a back and forth procedure. Blend and then add more of your light or dark value as needed.
Under the Tail -- Gently blend the underside of the tail. You may have to add more Primary Blue along the edge of the tail feathers and blend them into the shadow on the right side, leaving more blue showing on the left side. Add a bit of White at the top, where the body of the bird meets the tail, and blend it until it turns gray. This whole area is in shadow so there isn't much detail.

Eastern Bluebird

(9)

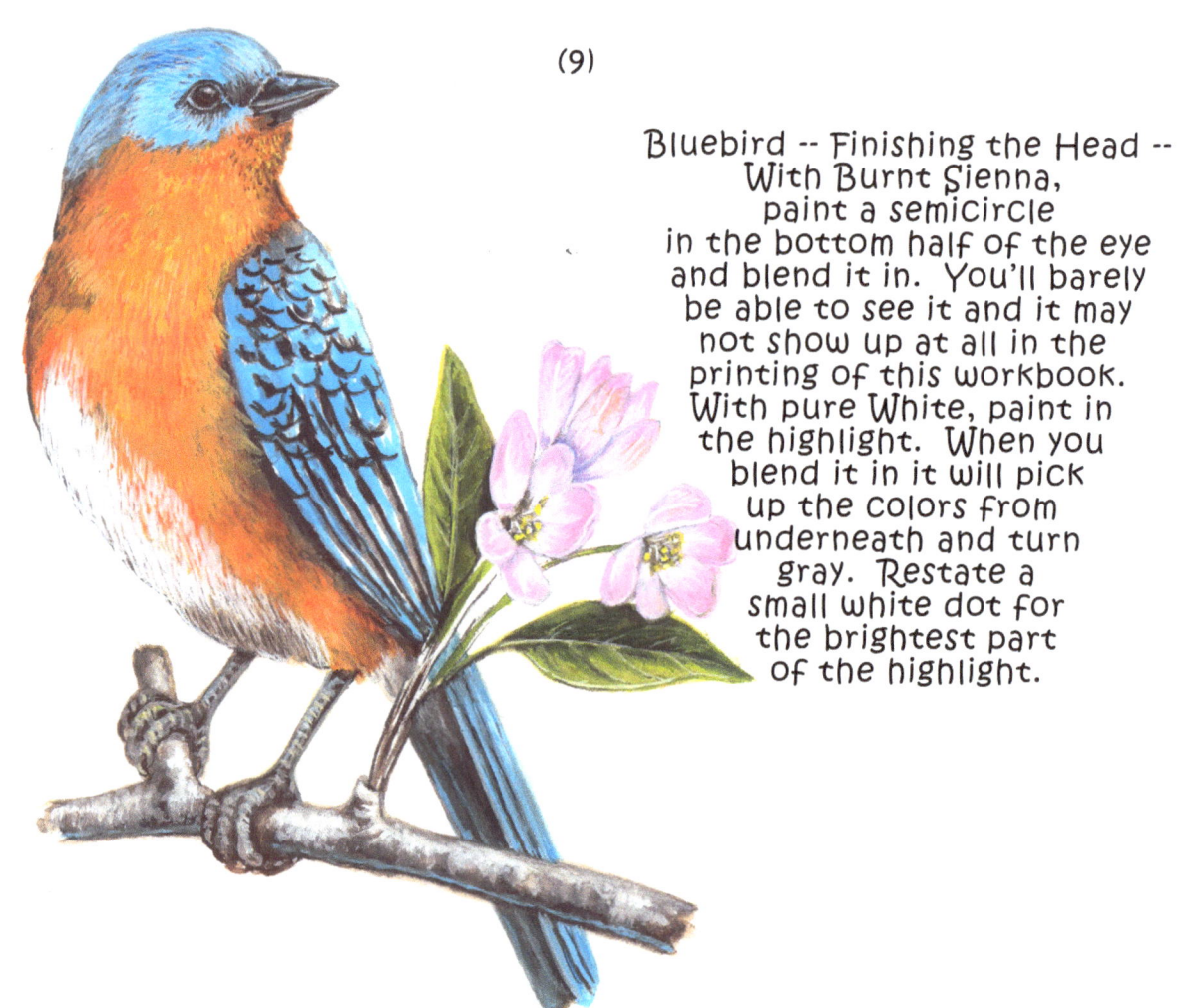

Bluebird -- Finishing the Head --
With Burnt Sienna,
paint a semicircle
in the bottom half of the eye
and blend it in. You'll barely
be able to see it and it may
not show up at all in the
printing of this workbook.
With pure White, paint in
the highlight. When you
blend it in it will pick
up the colors from
underneath and turn
gray. Restate a
small white dot for
the brightest part
of the highlight.

With your tiniest brush, use White barely tinted with Spectrum Blue
to paint fine strokes on the Bluebird's head, going in the
direction of the feather pattern. If your strokes are fine
enough you wont have to blend. The forehead should be
a little lighter because this is where the light strikes the feathers.
Because the lower layer blue will bleed into the White the bird
wont lok like it has a white head.
Tail -- To finish the right side of the tail, the part in the light,
use White tinted with Primay Blue to paint in the long tail
feahters. Use Burnt Umber mixed with Ultramarine Blue
to paint in the shaded lines and gently blend off the hard edges.
The Wing -- With your dark Burnt Umber and Ultramarine mixture,
paint in narrow lines to denote where the feathers go.

Eastern Bluebird

(10)

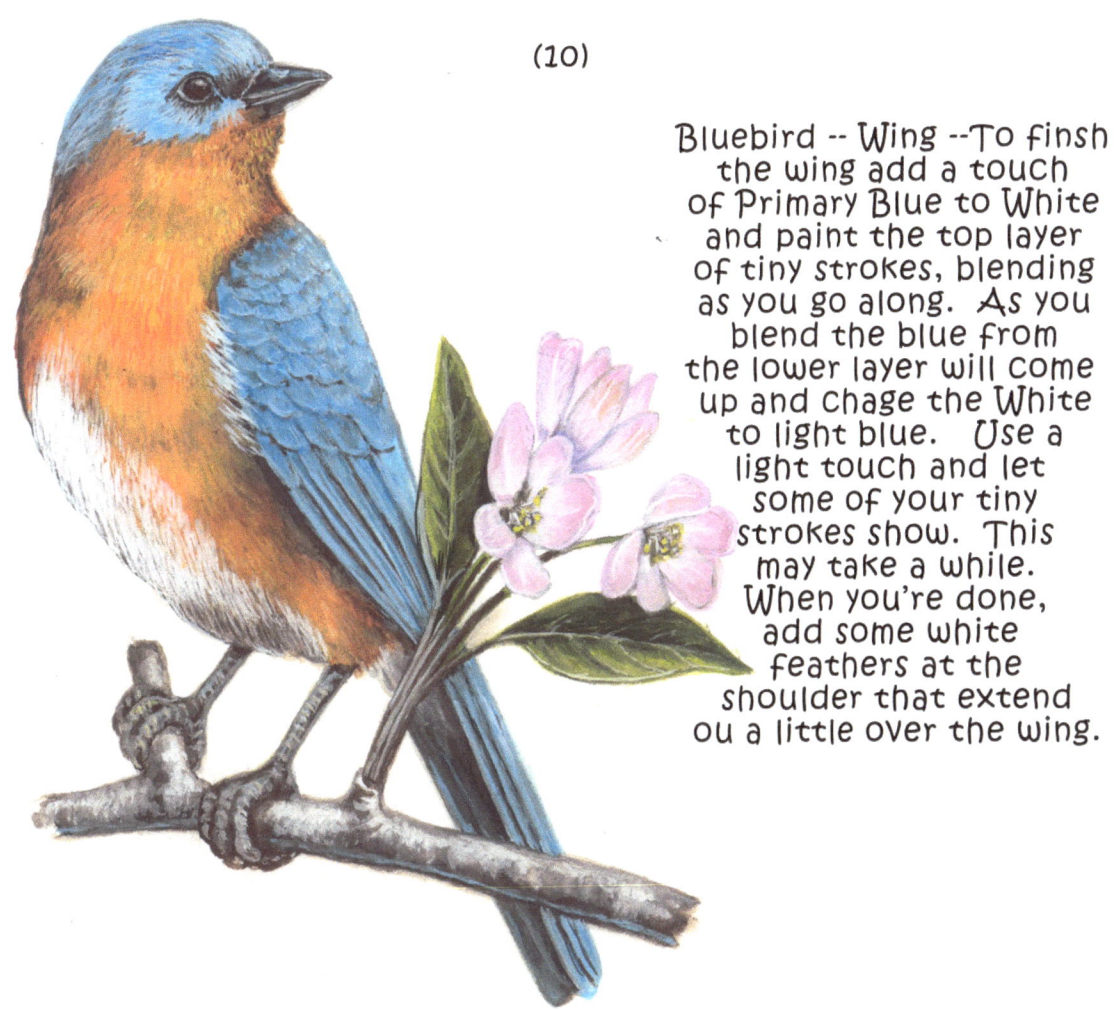

Bluebird -- Wing --To finsh the wing add a touch of Primary Blue to White and paint the top layer of tiny strokes, blending as you go along. As you blend the blue from the lower layer will come up and chage the White to light blue. Use a light touch and let some of your tiny strokes show. This may take a while. When you're done, add some white feathers at the shoulder that extend ou a little over the wing.

Stems -- Since the stems go over the Bluebird we've saved them for last. They have to show up against the bird. Use the Burnt Umber and Ultramarine Blue mixture to paint the right side of the stems and White to paint the left side. Blend a little.

If you haven't been softening the outside edges of the bird as you've been going along now is the time to do it. You don't want the Bluebird to look pasted on the paper.

Now, step back and check the values, colors and details on your work. You may want to lighten or darken an area or make other adjustments. Put it away for a few days and come back to it with fresh eyes!

Eastern Meadowlark
(Sturnella magna)

Colors Used: Permanent White, Burnt Umber, Ultramarine Blue,
Olive Green, Opera Pink, Burnt Sienna, Spectrum Yellow

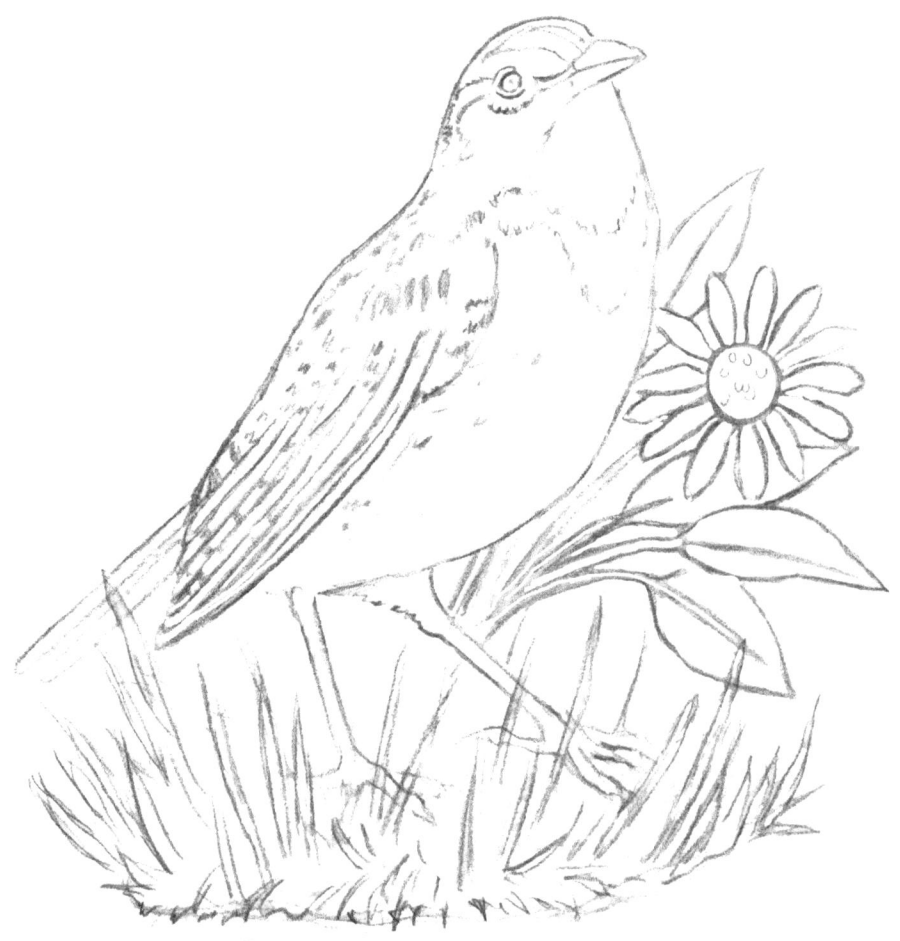

Use this sheet to transfer the image to your sheet of hot press
watercolor paper or illustration board.

Eastern Meadowlark

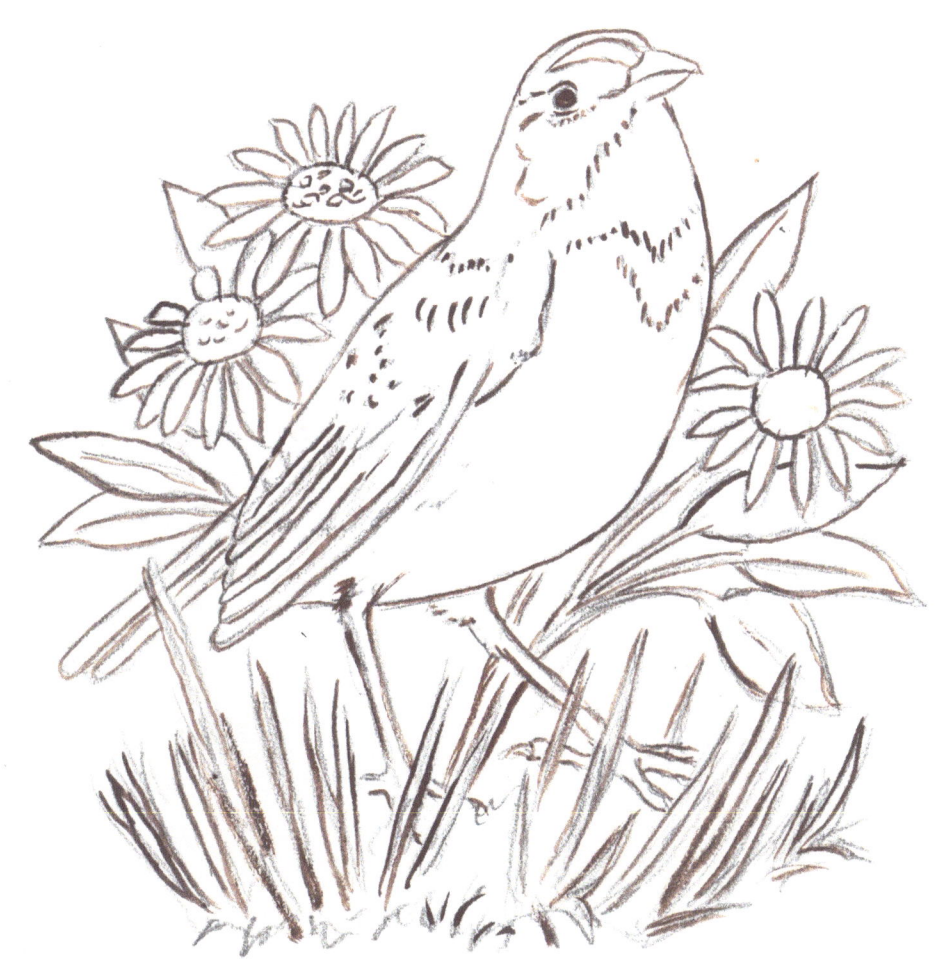

(1)

Transfer the drawing of the Meadowlark to your hot press watercolor
paper or smooth illustration board. With a thin, dark
mixture of Burnt Umber and Ultramarine Blue, paint over
your pencil lines to keep them intact when you start
layering on gouache. If you think your pencil lines are
dark enough you can skip this step.

Eastern Meadowlark

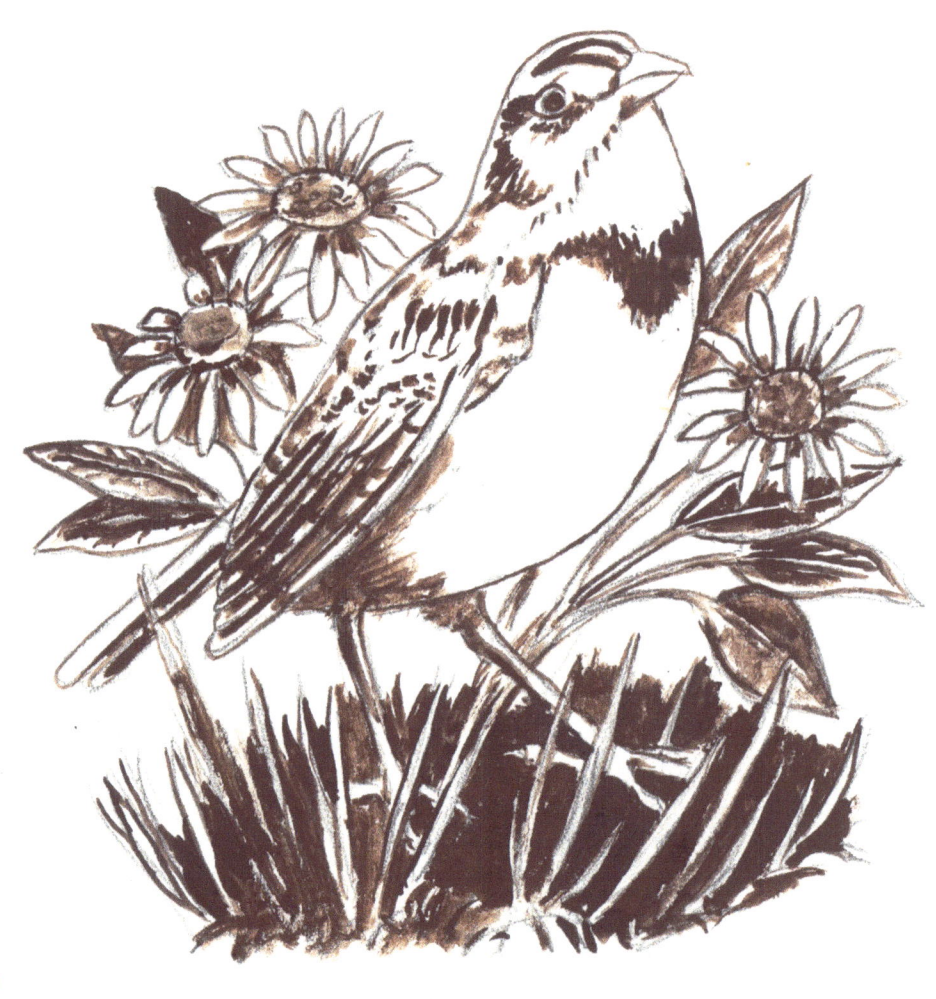

(2)

The dark value underpainting -- With a thin wash of a mixture of Burnt Umber and Ultramarine Blue, paint in the darkest places in the painting of the Meadowlark. Because the yellow color on the Meadowlark is relatively bright the underpainting won't cover the whole bird -- just where the darkest areas will be. A dark underpainting would dull the brightness of the yellow.

Eastern Meadowlark

(3)

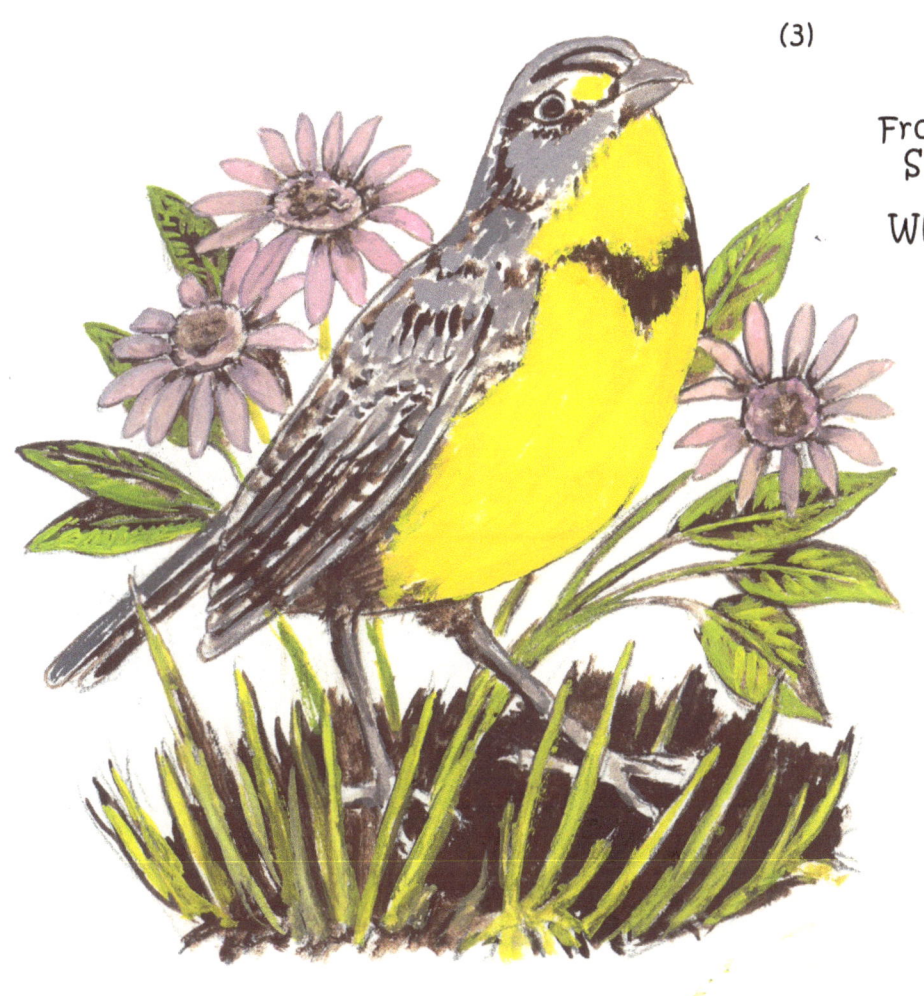

Front of Bird -- Use
Spectrum Yellow
mixed with
White to paint the
front of the
bird and the
small patch
on its face.

Coneflowers -- Mix Opera Rose with White and just a small amount of
medium gray (Burnt Umber, Ultramarine Blue and White) to tone
down the brightness of the hue a little. Roughly paint in
the petals of the flowers, stroking from the center outward.

Leaves and Grass-- Add a little Olive Green to Spectrum Yellow and White
and paint the next layer on the leaves. Make your strokes
on the leaves go from the center vein outward toward the edges of the leaves.
Dont worry about being too careful. The painting will look "messy at
this point. Use the same mixture to roughly pain in the grass,

Eastern Meadowlark

(4)

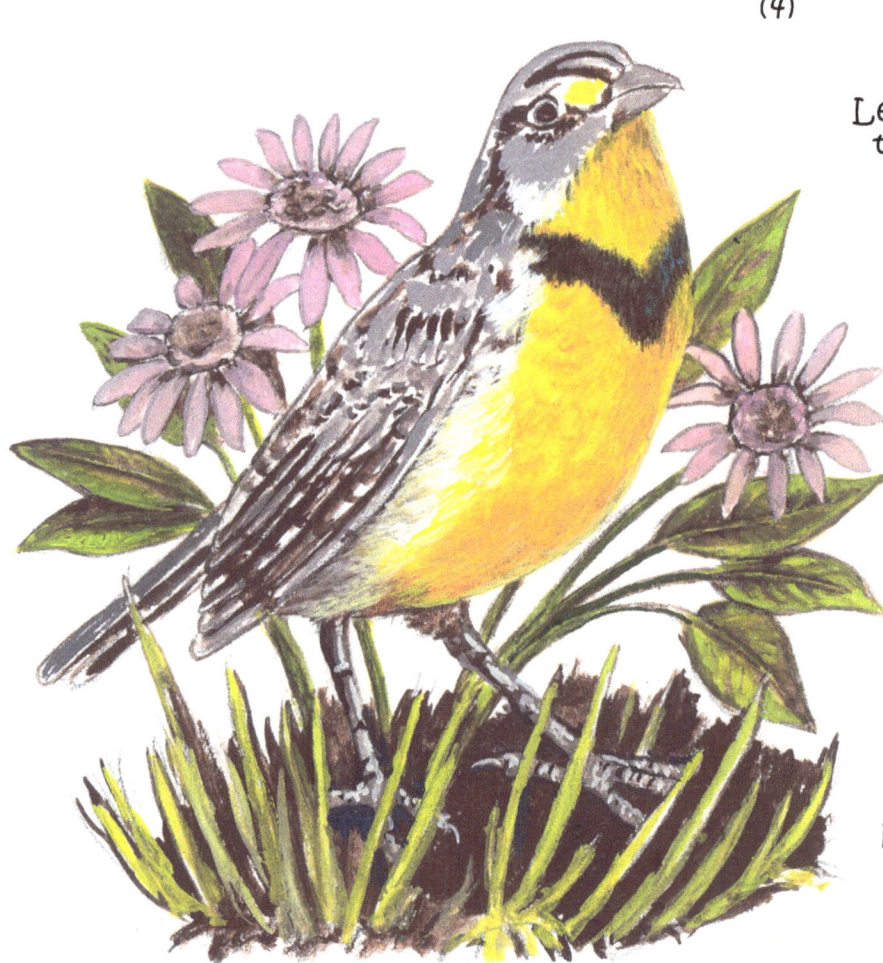

Leaves -- Gently blend the colors together where they meet, making smooth transitions.

Legs & Feet -- With the darkest value of Burnt Umber and Ultramarine Blue, paint arcs around the legs and toes, following their contours. With pure White, paint in the highlights as in the illustration.

Bird's Breast -- With a mixture of Burnt Sienna, Spectrum Yellow, White and a touch of Olive Green, paint the texture on the breast of the Meadowlark using strokes that go in the direction of the feather pattern. Gently blend them in. Make the area under the beak and the underside of the belly darker. When you make your strokes make sure that you let the lower layer of yellow show through in places.

The Dark "Necklace" -- With your darkest value paint the necklace. Make tiny strokes extending into the yellow above and below the dark areas. Gently blend the edges. On the right side paint small strokes of Primary Blue and blend them in. On the left side add a few strokes of white and blend them in. With pure, thick White, paint the area next to where the chest and wing feathers meet. You may have to add several layers of White before it will cover properly. Gently blend the area where the white and yellow meet to make smooth transitions.

Eastern Meadowlark

(5)

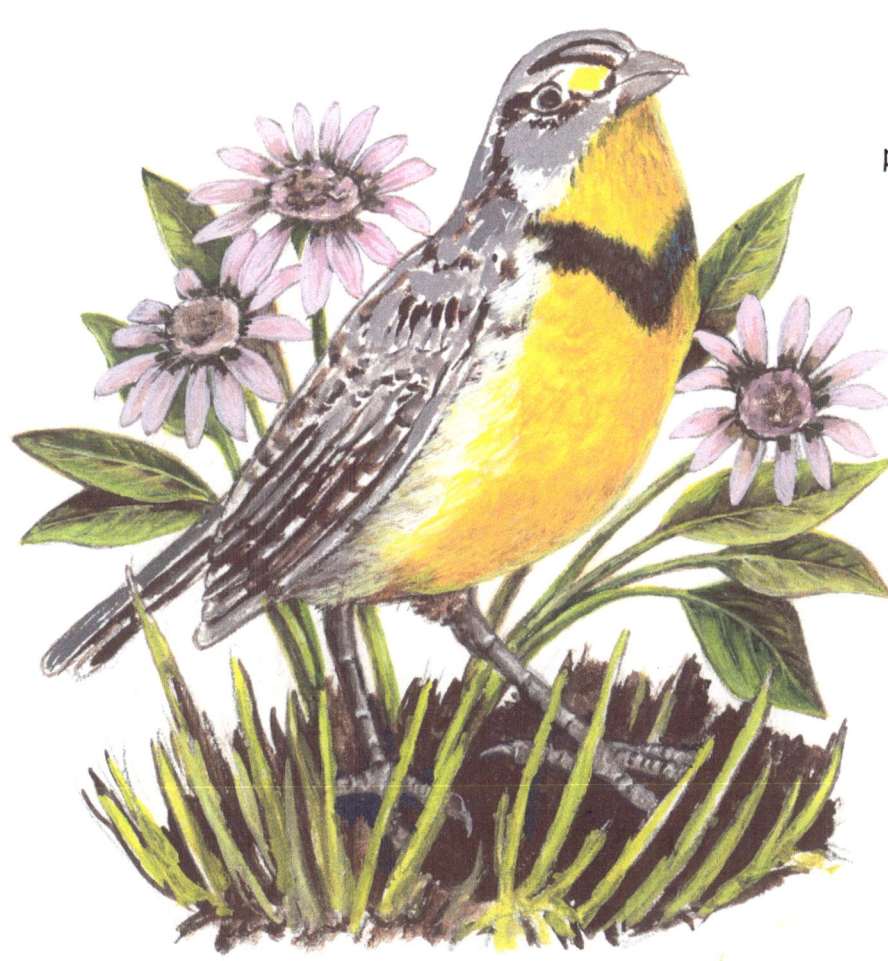

Legs & Feet -- Once the grass has been painted in you won't be able to see much of the legs and feet so don't go into too much detail. With a damp brush, gently blend the light and dark together where they meet. You may have to add more of the white and reblend.

Leaves & Stems -- Paint another layer of gouache on the leaves and stems, this time with a light value mixture of Spectrum Yellow, White and a touch of Olive Green. It will look too light when you paint it on the leaves but remember -- as soon as you start blending the color will darken. You may have to add more as you go along and then reblend. Use a very light yellow (Spectrum Yellow and White) and your smallest brush tip to paint in the veins.

Coneflowers -- With White barely tinted with Opera Pink, paint the petals on the flowers. Make your strokes go from the inside of the flower outward to the edges. Put more White toward the outside ends of the petals. Let some of the lower layer of pink show through to give the petals depth. Make sure you almost cover the dark lines on the edges of the petals. Mix Burnt Sienna and Olive Green and paint the shadows on the petals, where they attach to the center.

Eastern Meadowlark

(6)

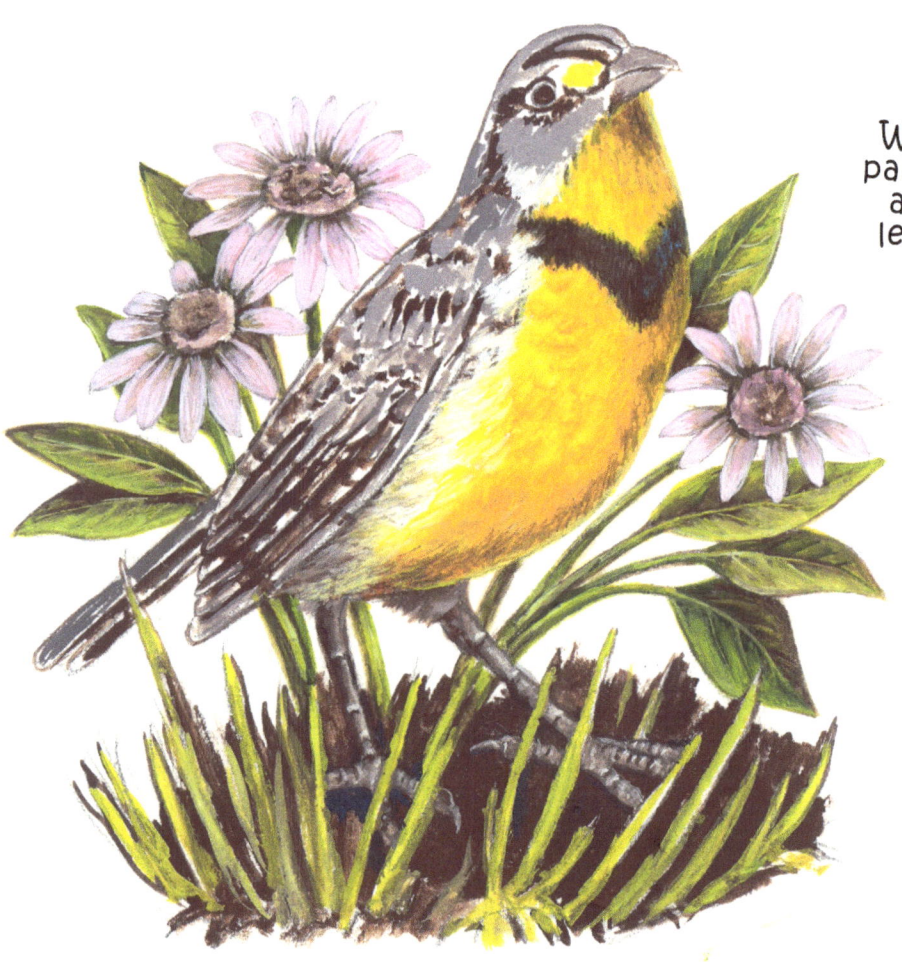

Upper Legs --
With a dark value,
paint the feathering
at the top of the
legs. Add a touch
of White to
make a small
highight area
on the top
of the left
leg and
blend it.

Final Shadows in Breast -- With Burnt Umber, shadow the right side of the breast and under the beak by painting small strokes following the contour of the bird. Very gently blend the hard edges off the strokes.

Coneflower Petals -- To finish the petals use White barely tinted with Opera Pink to paint very tiny strokes running from the center of the flower to the outside edges. Don't entirely cover the pink layer below. Some of the lower pink will mix with the white. You may have to add more White as you go along. Don't get too near the center. You still need to have a dark shadow there for when the center is painted. Make sure all your petals have smooth transitions -- no hard edges between the colors and values.

Eastern Meadowlark

(7)

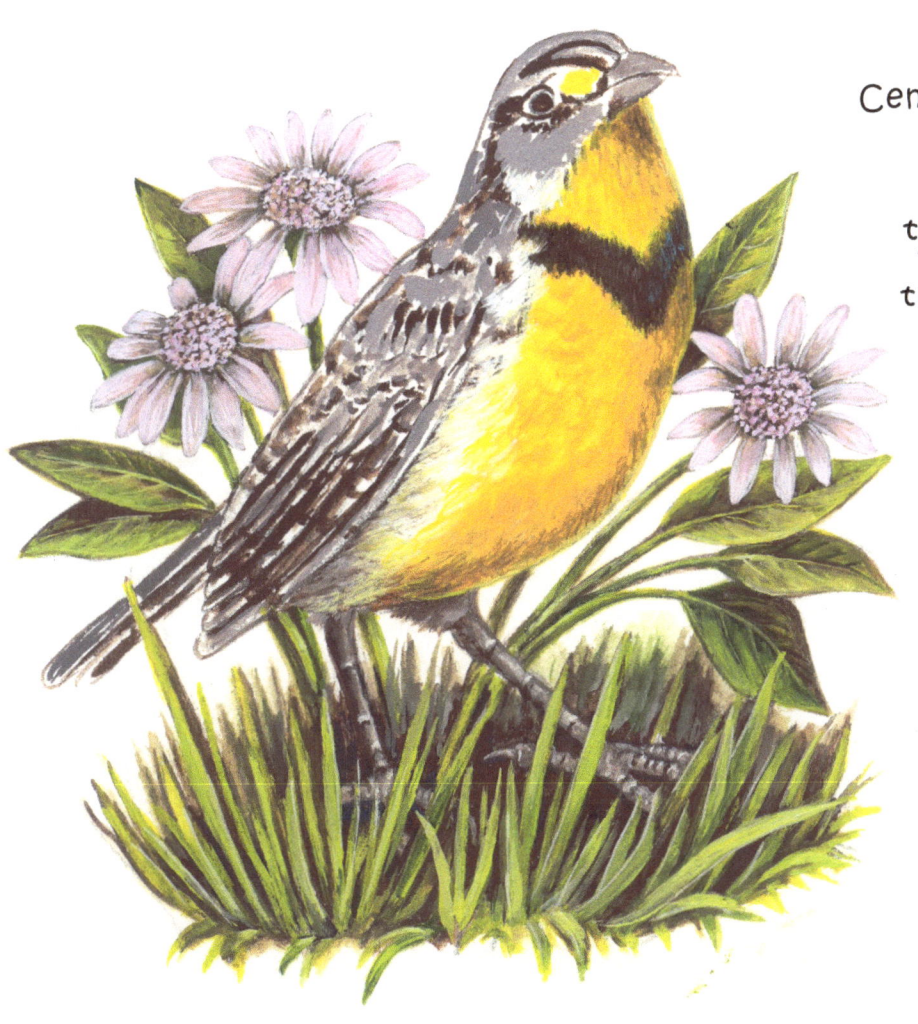

Centers of Flowers --
To finish the
flowers, tint
White with a
touch of Opera
Pink. Be sure
the paint is very
thick. Dot
it on the
centers of
the flowers.

Grass -- Mix a cool gray by adding White and a touch of Olive Green
to your Burnt Umber and Ultramarine Blue mixture. Paint in
a few blades of grass in the back. Things further away are less
distinct and cooler in hue. Mix Spectrum Yellow, White and
Olive Green to paint in the rest of the blades of grass.
Use more White to highlight some of the blades and some of your
darkest value to add some shadows to the blades. Blend
as you go along. Also, add a white line along the front edges of
some of the blades on the side that turns toward the front of
the painting.

Eastern Meadowlark

(8)

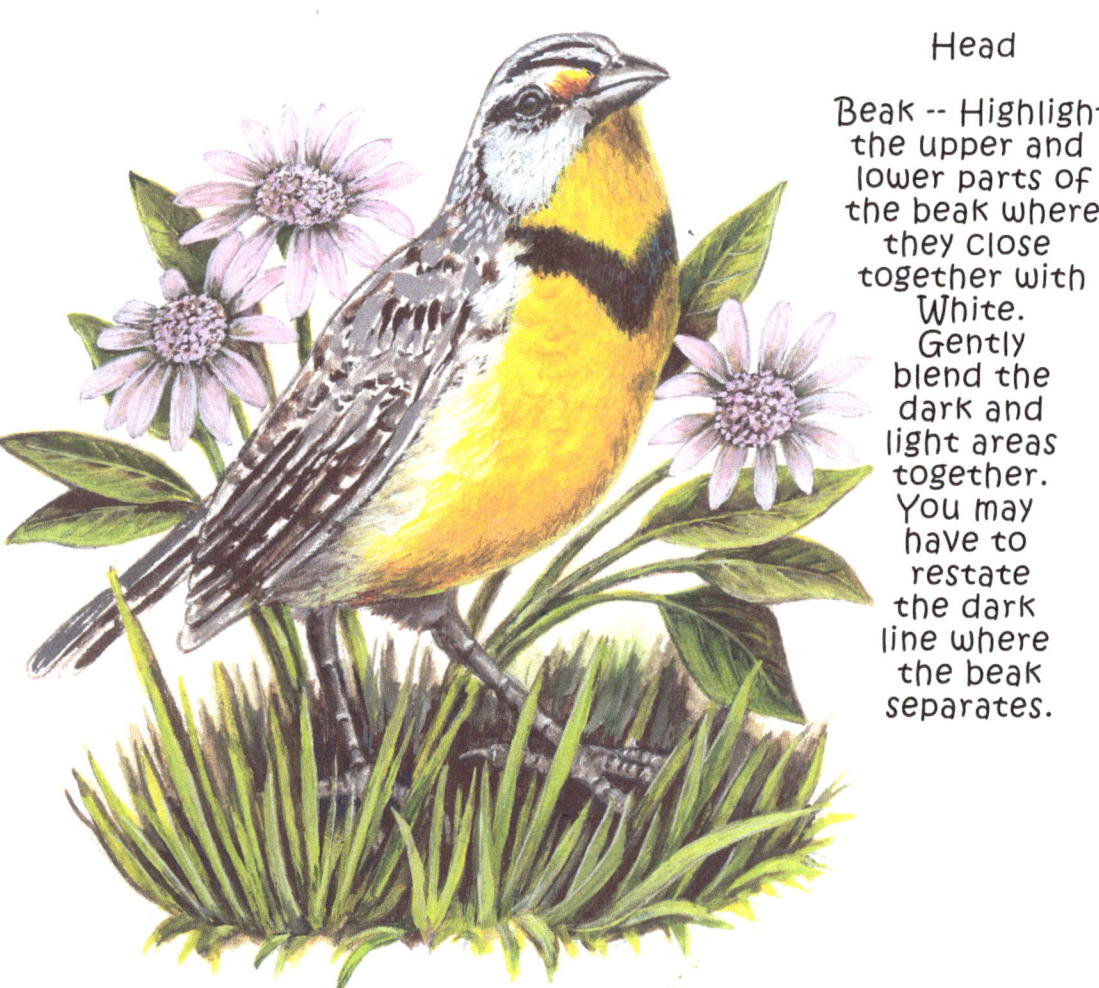

Head

Beak -- Highlight the upper and lower parts of the beak where they close together with White. Gently blend the dark and light areas together. You may have to restate the dark line where the beak separates.

Eye -- Shape the eye with your darkest value of Burnt Umber and Ultramarine Blue mixed together. Paint a very narrow white line around it. With Burnt Sienna mixed with Spectrum Yellow, paint a semicircle in the lower half of the eye. Blend ever so slightly. Use White to add the highlight. Some of the dark color from underneath will mix with the White and make it gray so you may have to add an even smaller dot of White. You want the outside edge of the highlight to be softened a little but leave a small, very bright highlight in its center.

White patch on head -- With pure White start detailing the head. Make your strokes go in the direction of the feather pattern. Let some of the lower dark layer show through. Some of it will immediately mix with the White, creating subtle variations in color and tone. If the White gets too dark just add more. Also, add a few strokes of Burnt Sienna where the beak meets the head.

Eastern Meadowlark

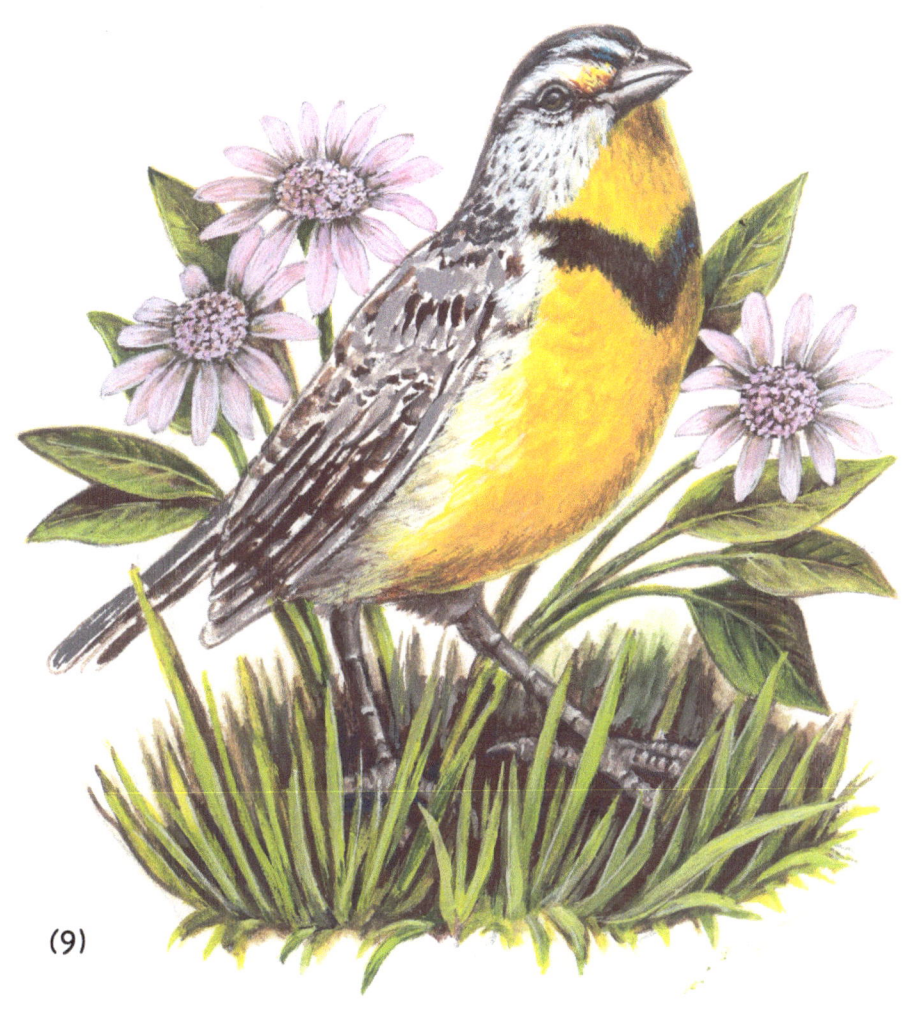

(9)

Head -- With your darkest value, paint in the stripes and dots on the head. You'll probably have to add more White as you go along. Keep checking your values. Always make your strokes go in the direction of the feather pattern and blend off the hard edges. This is a back and forth process. Also add some strokes of Spectrum Yellow mixed with White over the Burnt Umber where the back meets the head.

Eastern Meadowlark

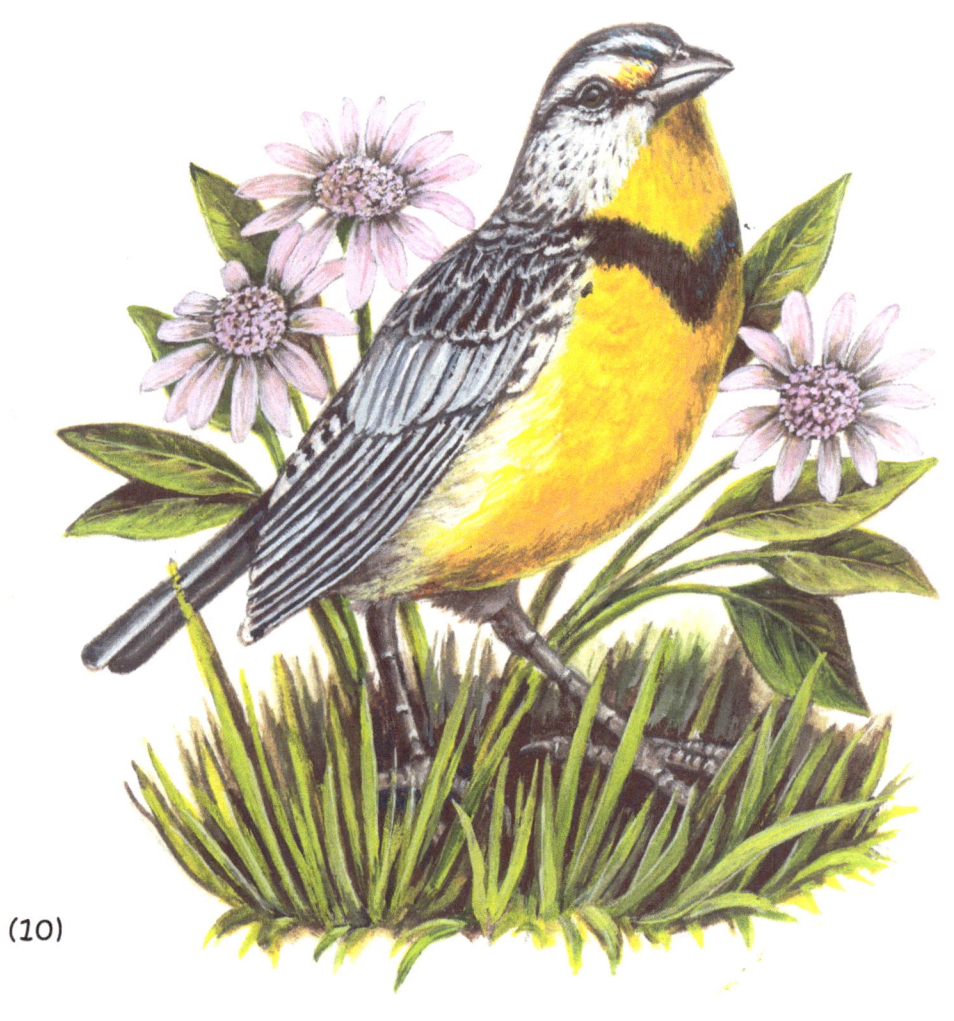

(10)

Back & Wings -- These last steps will be done using thick, pure White and the dark Burnt Umber and Ultramarine Blue mixture. The feathers need to be carefully organized into the correct pattern. Switch from White to your dark value gouache and blend to make smooth transitions between the values. Remember that the feathers curve around the body. Place the feathers in the right position before you start detailing them.

Tail -- Blend the hard edges on the tail feathers to soften them.

Eastern Meadowlark

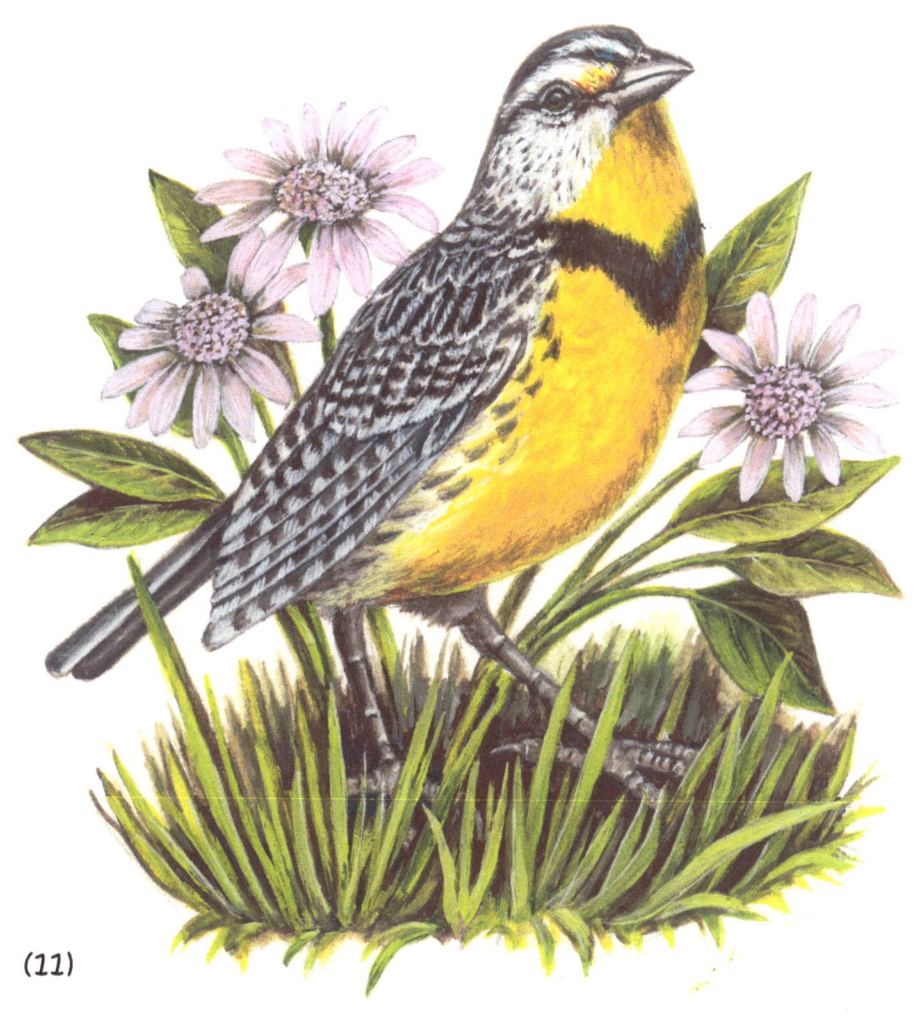

(11)

Back & Wings -- With your darkest value, paint the bars on the feathers. Each one will have to be blended in so this will take a while. With your smallest brush, use pure White to paint tiny strokes on the edges of the feathers. If you make them small enough you won't have to blend them. Also, paint the dark triangular shapes on the sides of the chest within the yellow area. Blend them in.

Now, stand back and check your values, color and details. Make sure you have a full range of values so the bird "reads" correctly and the image is sharp with both very dark and very light areas. That will make it more visually intersting. Put the painting away for a few days and go back to it with fresh eyes before you call it done. And you can always go back to it weeks, months or even years later to make adjustments. That's one of the beauties of gouache!

American Robin
(Turdus migratorius)

Colors Used: Permanent White, Burnt Umber, Ultramarine Blue, Olive Green, Marigold Yellow, Burnt Sienna, Primary Blue, Spectrum Yellow

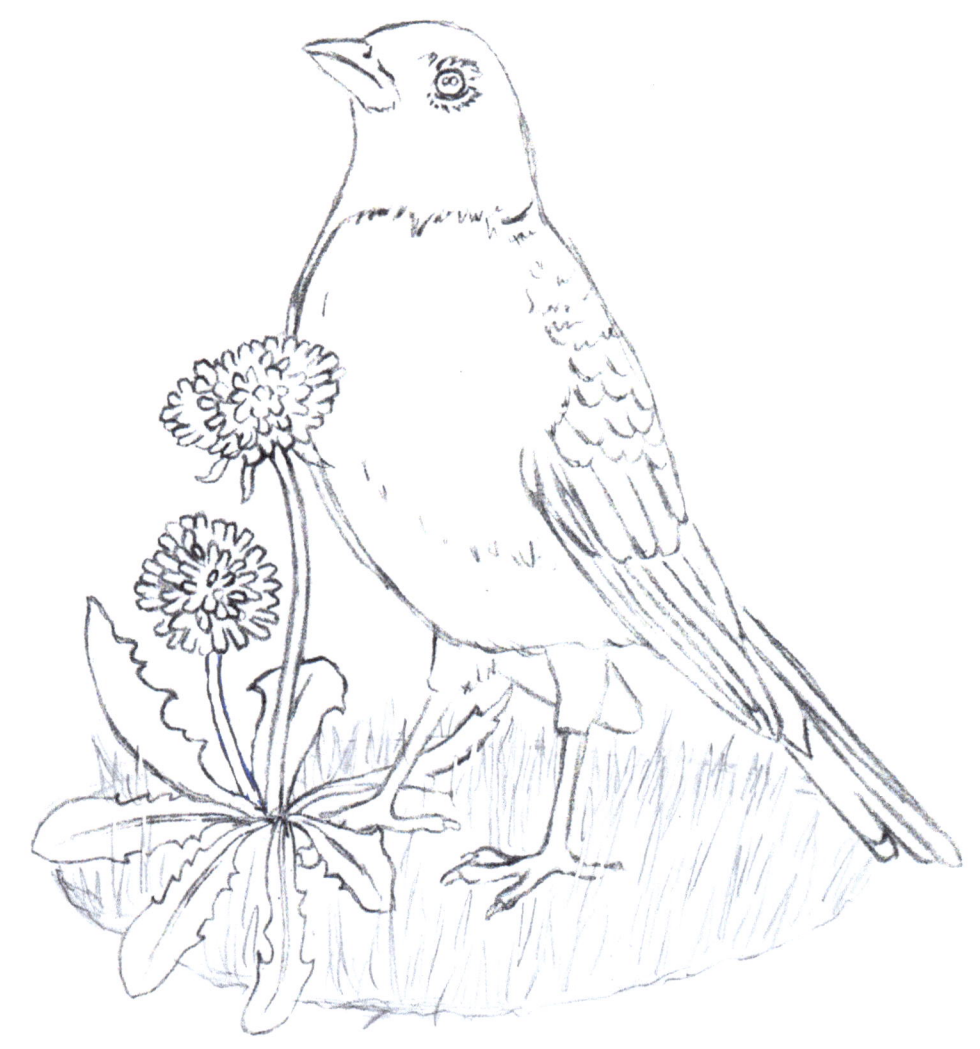

Use this sheet to transfer the image to your sheet of hot press watercolor paper or illustration board.

American Robin

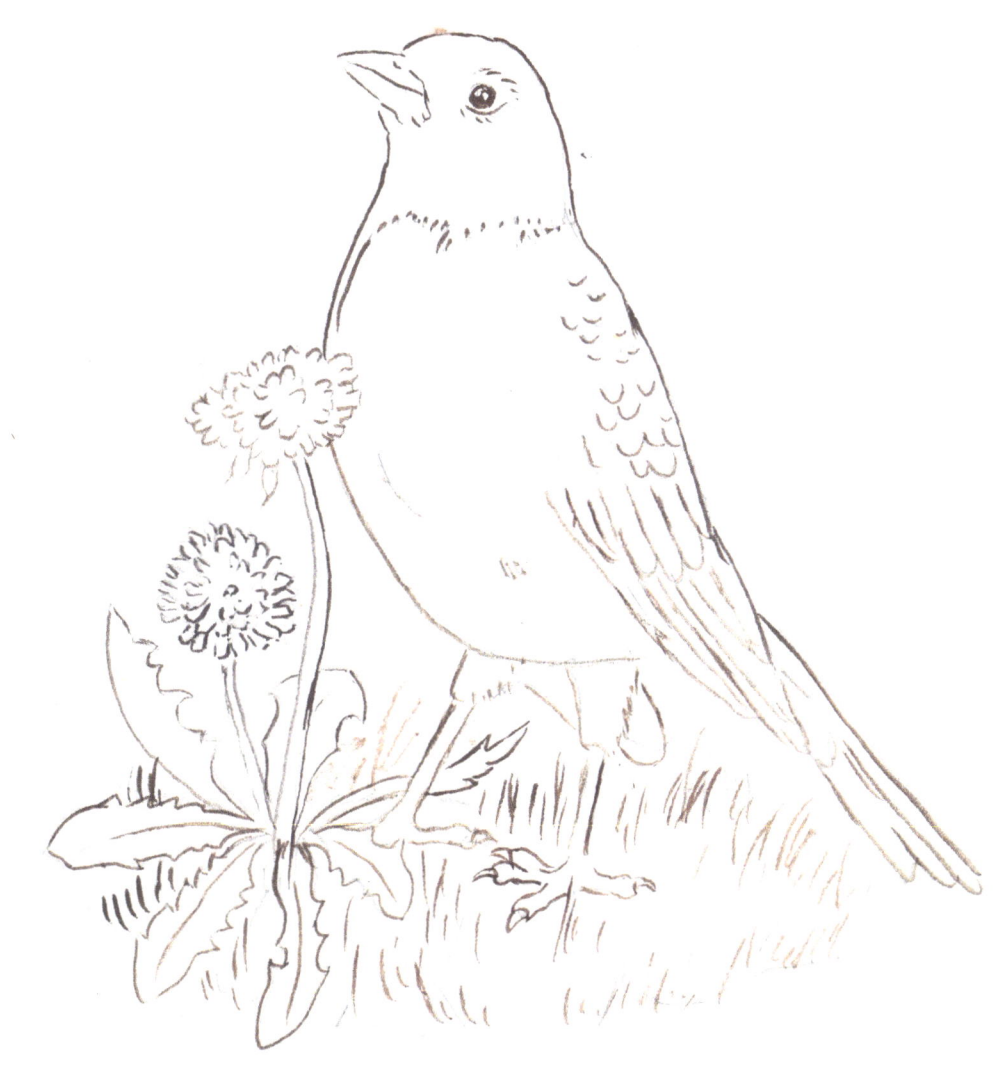

(1)

Transfer the drawing of the Robin to your hot press watercolor paper or smooth illustration board. With a thin, dark mixture of Burnt Umber and Ultramarine Blue, paint over your pencil lines to keep them intact when you start layering on gouache. If you think your pencil lines are dark enough you can skip this step.

American Robin

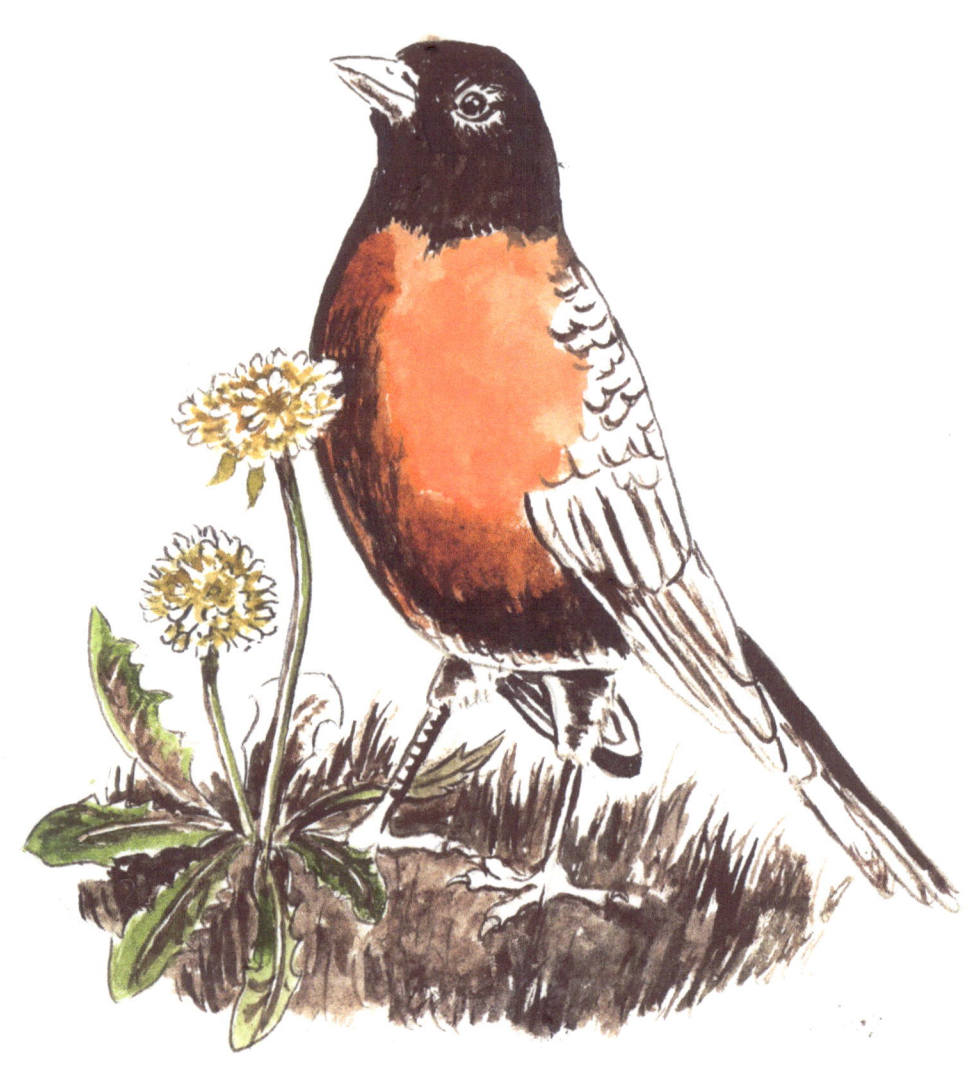

(2)

Using the dark, thin mixture of Burnt Umber and Ultramarine Blue, paint in the darkest areas of the painting. Don't worry about being too exact -- the painting will look a little messy at this stage. With a thin wash of Burnt Sienna, paint in the middle value on the left side and lower portion of the bird's body. Use Marigold Yellow to paint in the brightest part of the chest. Dandelion -- With a thin wash of Olive Green, paint the right side of the stems and the medium value areas of the leaves. With a thin wash of Burnt Sienna mixed with a touch of Olive Green, rough in the flower heads.

American Robin

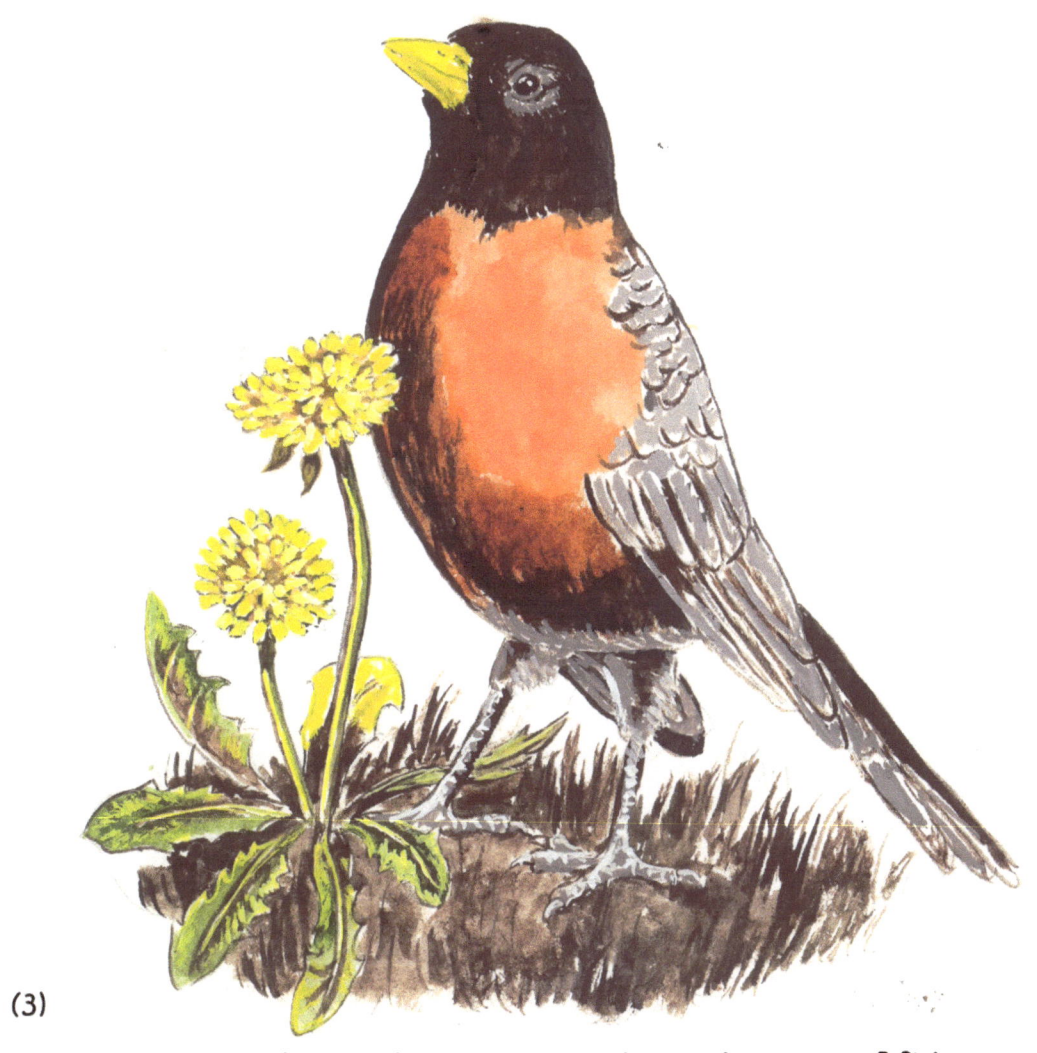

(3)

The Robin -- Add a little of your dark mixture to White and paint over the parts of the bird that have not been covered, mostly the wings and underside. Use Spectrum Yellow (this color is a bit transparent) to paint the bill. The yellow should be a thin wash so your lines show through. Any time you add white the paint becaomes much more opaque but don't make this layer very thick.

Dandelion -- With Spectrum Yellow mixed with White, paint the left sides of the 2 stems. Also begin adding the same color to the leaves of the dandelion. On the top flower head, add shadows on the 2 little leaves that are hanging down with your dark value. With White tinted with Spectrum Yellow paint the petals of the flower head. Stroke from the center outward to the edges of the petals.

Legs -- Use Pure White to detail the legs and feet as in the illustration.

Everything is still pretty rough at this stage.

American Robin

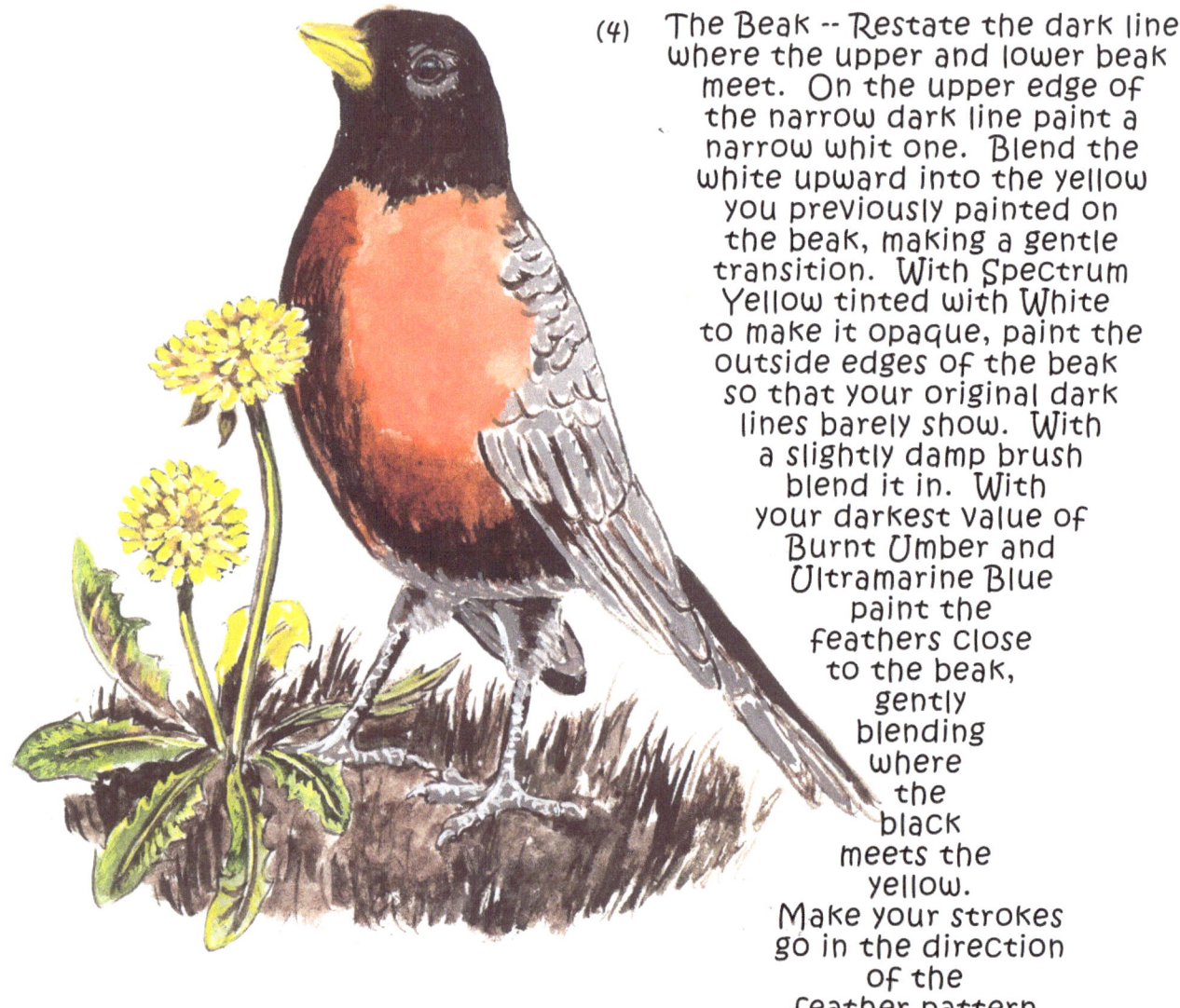

(4) The Beak -- Restate the dark line where the upper and lower beak meet. On the upper edge of the narrow dark line paint a narrow whit one. Blend the white upward into the yellow you previously painted on the beak, making a gentle transition. With Spectrum Yellow tinted with White to make it opaque, paint the outside edges of the beak so that your original dark lines barely show. With a slightly damp brush blend it in. With your darkest value of Burnt Umber and Ultramarine Blue paint the feathers close to the beak, gently blending where the black meets the yellow. Make your strokes go in the direction of the feather pattern.

The Eye -- Make sure the shape of the eye is correct using your darkest value of Burnt Umber mixed with Ultramarine Blue. Paint the upper and lower rims of the eye with light gray made by adding White to your dark mixture. With the tiniest bit of Burnt Sienna paint a semicircle on the lower half of the eye, gently blending it in. You'll barely be able to see it. Mix Primary Blue with White and paint a highlight at the top of the eye. Blend it in. Very carefully put a small pure white highliht over the blue one you just painted. Blend the white highlight only around the edges. We're working with very small elements here and it may be necessary to do the steps over again until you get the right balance of lights and darks when you blend.

American Robin

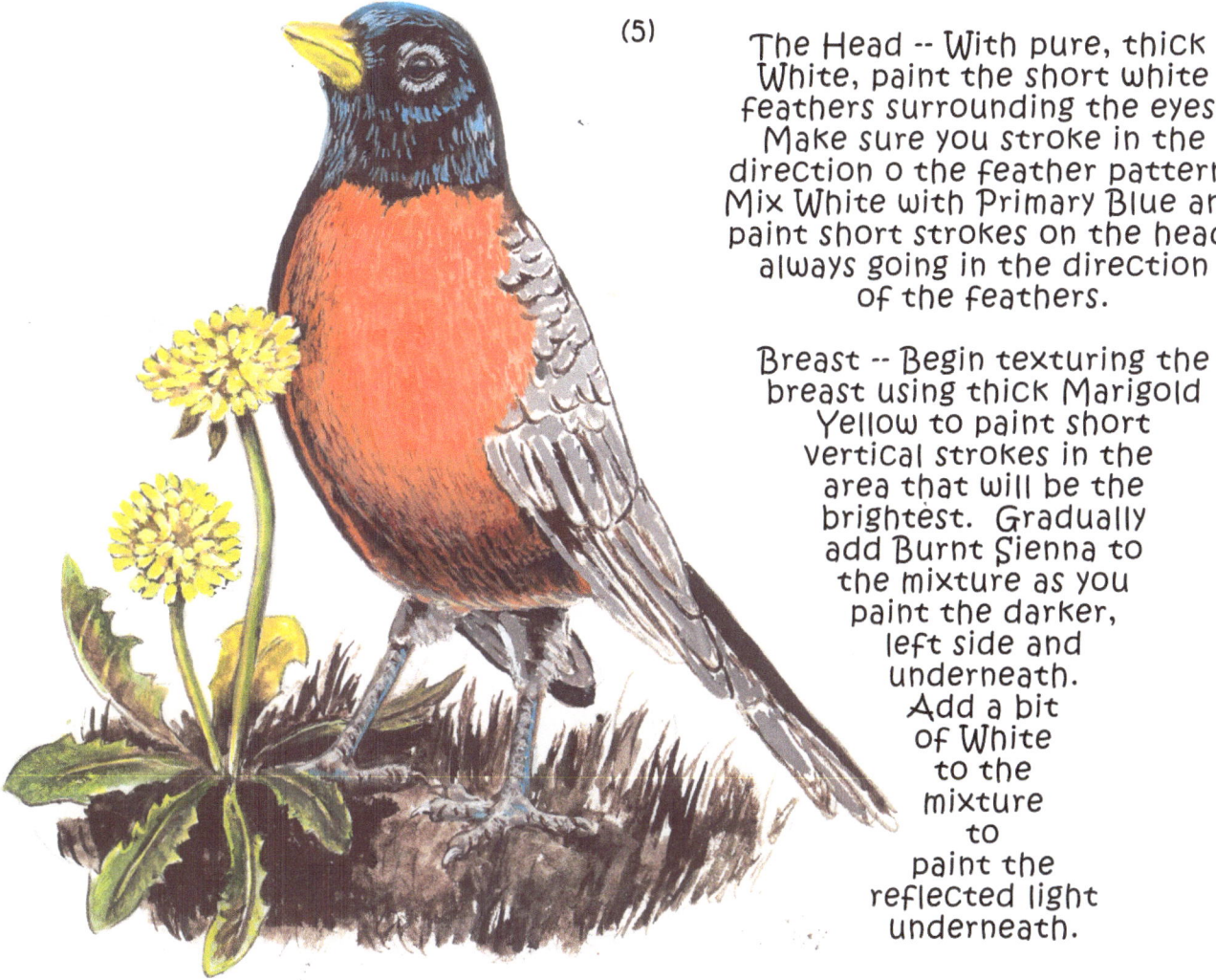

(5) The Head -- With pure, thick White, paint the short white feathers surrounding the eyes. Make sure you stroke in the direction o the feather pattern. Mix White with Primary Blue and paint short strokes on the head, always going in the direction of the feathers.

Breast -- Begin texturing the breast using thick Marigold Yellow to paint short vertical strokes in the area that will be the brightest. Gradually add Burnt Sienna to the mixture as you paint the darker, left side and underneath. Add a bit of White to the mixture to paint the reflected light underneath.

Dandelion -- With a slightly damp brush, blend the edges of the different areas of color on the leaves together to make smooth transitions. Darken the shadow areas under the dandelion leaves with your dark mixture. of Burnt Umber and Ultramarine Blue. Begin to blend the color areas on the leaves together. They'll still be too dark. We'll add the lighter layer later.

Legs -- With a slightly damp brush, blend the light and dark values you painted before. You may have to add more dark or light as you go along and reblend. With Primary Blue tinted with Whte, paint a narrow blue line on the right side of each leg and blend it in a little for reflected light.

American Robin

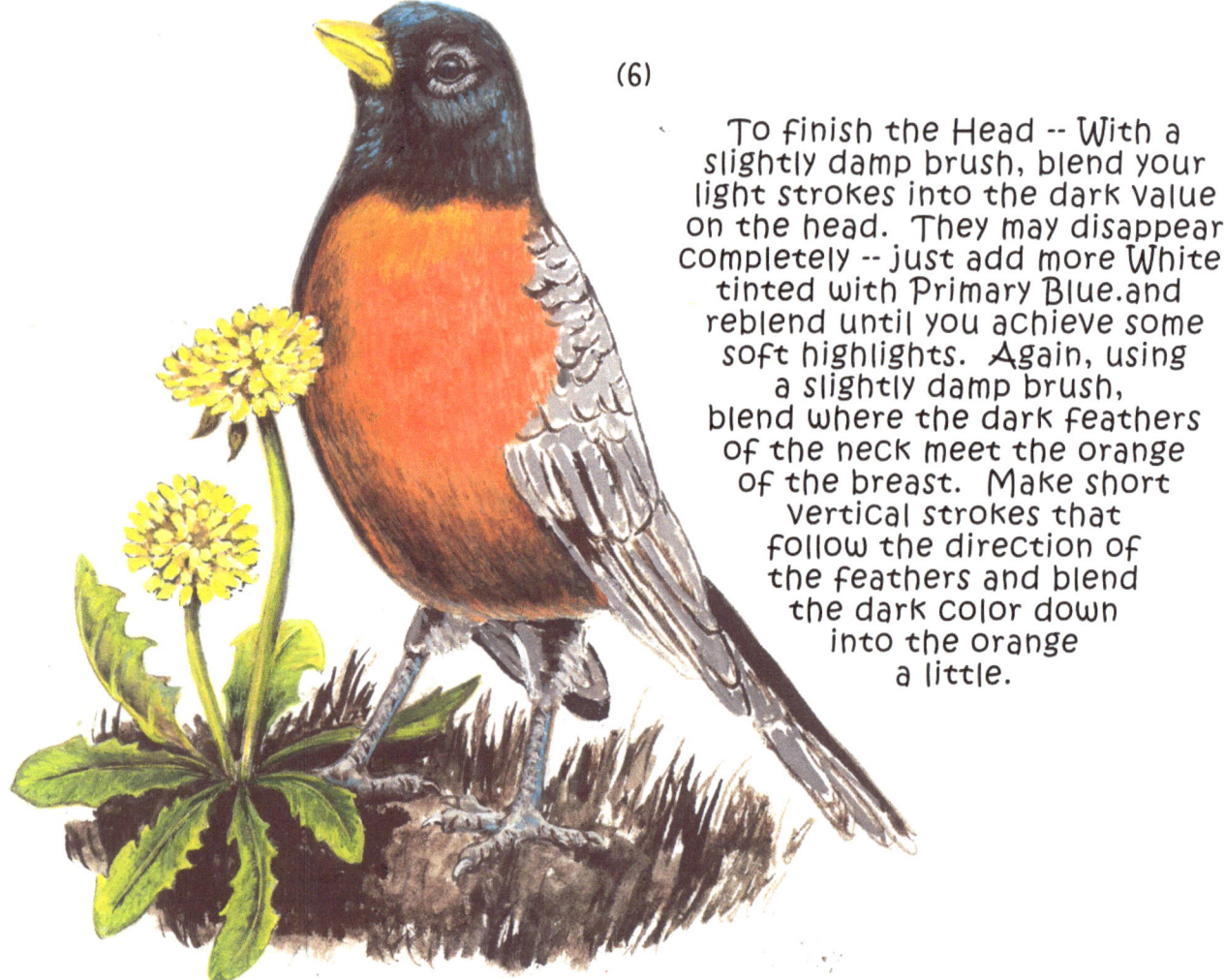

(6)

To finish the Head -- With a slightly damp brush, blend your light strokes into the dark value on the head. They may disappear completely -- just add more White tinted with Primary Blue.and reblend until you achieve some soft highlights. Again, using a slightly damp brush, blend where the dark feathers of the neck meet the orange of the breast. Make short vertical strokes that follow the direction of the feathers and blend the dark color down into the orange a little.

Breast -- Blend the strokes you painted on the breast. Don't blend your strokes out completely -- just soften them and let the lower layer show through in places. Avoid flat areas of color. Add some strokes of Primary Yellow to the very top portion of the breast to highlight that area. Blend your strokes. Add some subtle, scattered, vertical strokes of Burnt Umber and blend them in to help break up the large area of the bird's breast.

Dandelion Leaves -- The next layer for the leaves will be made by mixing Spectrum Yellow with the tiniest bit of Olive Green. Because this mixture is a little transparent you'll also have to add White. Be sure the gouache is a creamy consistency and brush it on the dandelion leaves. stroking from the center to the outside edges. It will seem too light but when you blend it in it will darken. Make the tips of the leaves lighter than the parts toward the center. You will probably have to paint on another layer of your light mixture on the tips.

American Robin

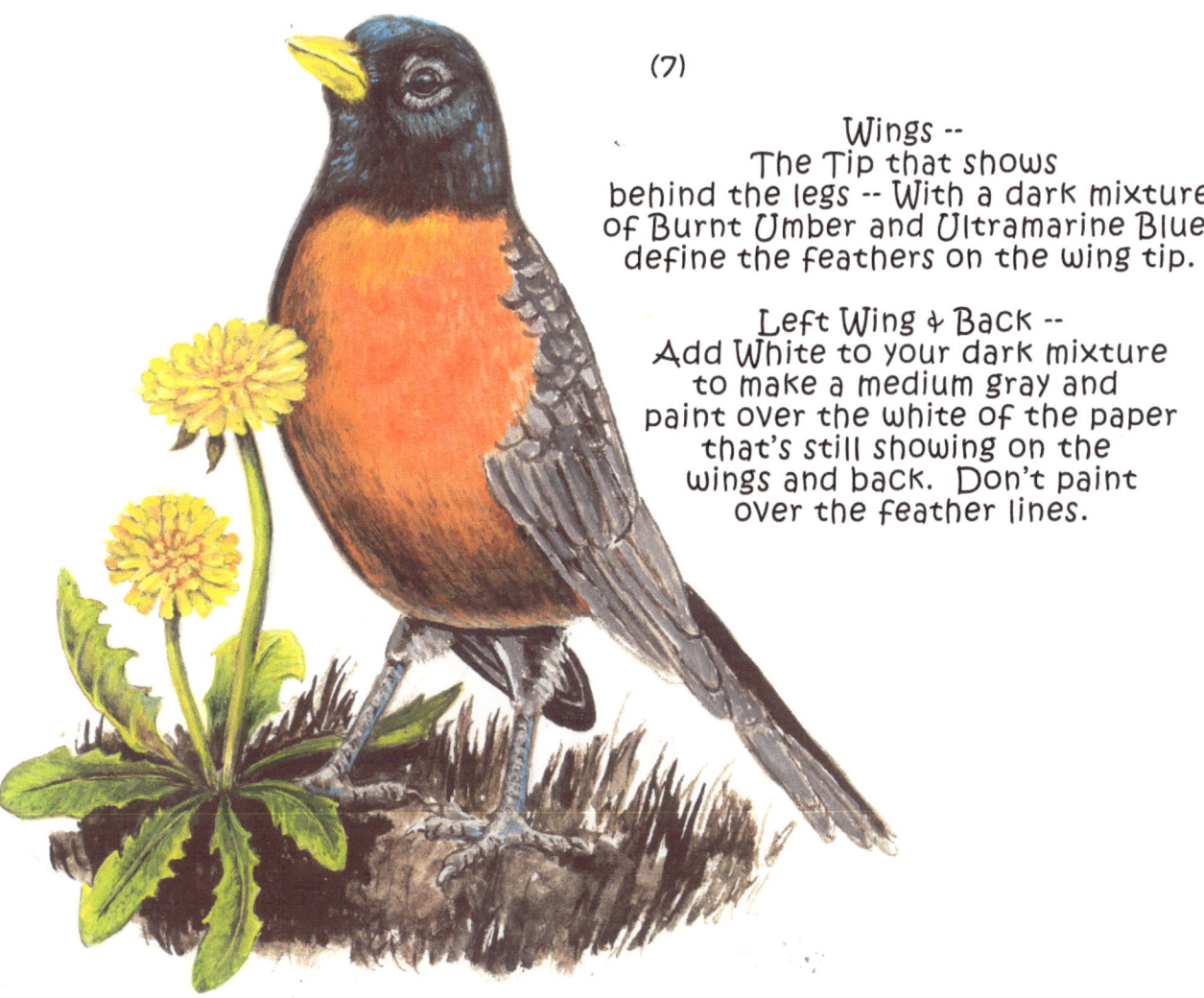

(7)

Wings --
The Tip that shows
behind the legs -- With a dark mixture
of Burnt Umber and Ultramarine Blue,
define the feathers on the wing tip.

Left Wing & Back --
Add White to your dark mixture
to make a medium gray and
paint over the white of the paper
that's still showing on the
wings and back. Don't paint
over the feather lines.

Dandelion Heads -- With a damp brush blend the colors in the little
petals. Use Burnt Sienna and add some more darks in the
shadow areas and blend.   Add White to Spectrum Yellow and
paint the tips of the petals. Blend to soften the edges and
make smooth transitions between the values.

American Robin

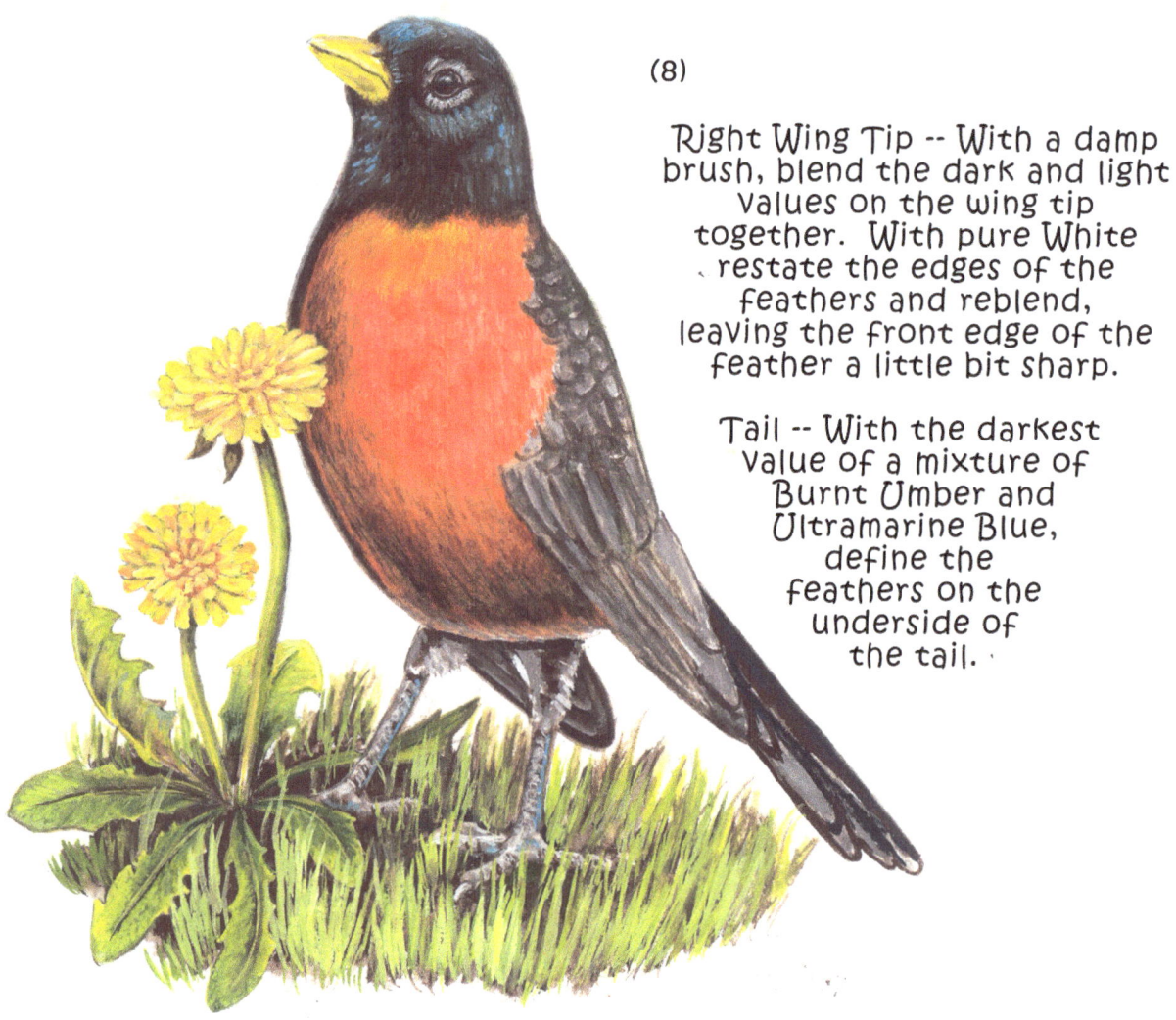

(8)

Right Wing Tip -- With a damp brush, blend the dark and light values on the wing tip together. With pure White restate the edges of the feathers and reblend, leaving the front edge of the feather a little bit sharp.

Tail -- With the darkest value of a mixture of Burnt Umber and Ultramarine Blue, define the feathers on the underside of the tail.

Back and Left Wing -- With a slightly damp brush, gently blend the darks into the lights you already painted on the back and wing. The wing will be too dark but you'll be adding another finishing layer so this is normal

Grass -- For the grass make a light value mixture of Spectrum Yellow barely tinted with Olive Green. Because this yellow is somewhat transparent you'll need to add enough white to make it opaque. Use upward strokes to paint the grass, painting the blades in front first and working backwards. Blend your strokes gently. Then add another layer of your light yellow mixture on the blades in front to bring them forward. Blend slightly.

American Robin

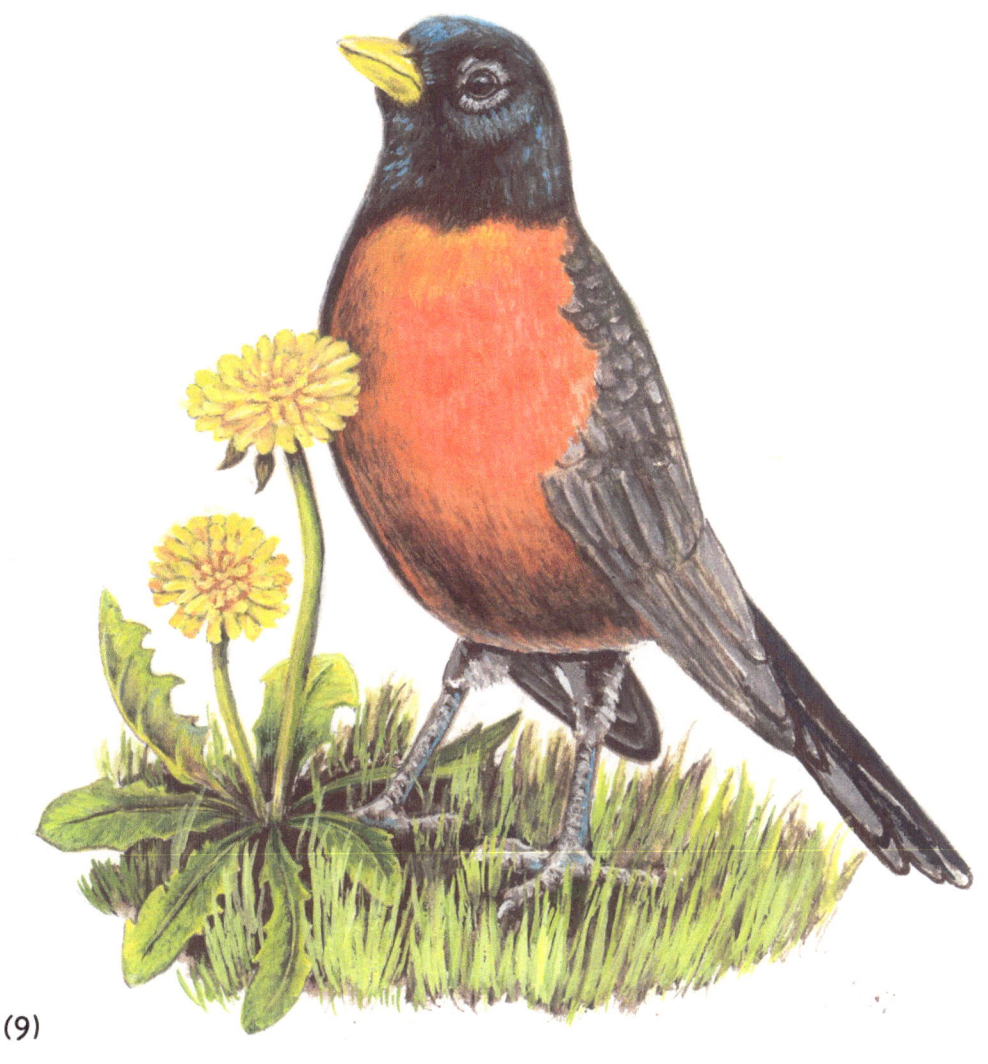

(9)

Back, Wings, Underside of Tail -- With pure White, paint in the next layer of gouache.

Upper Legs -- Also with pure White, paint in the feathers on the upper legs.

American Robin

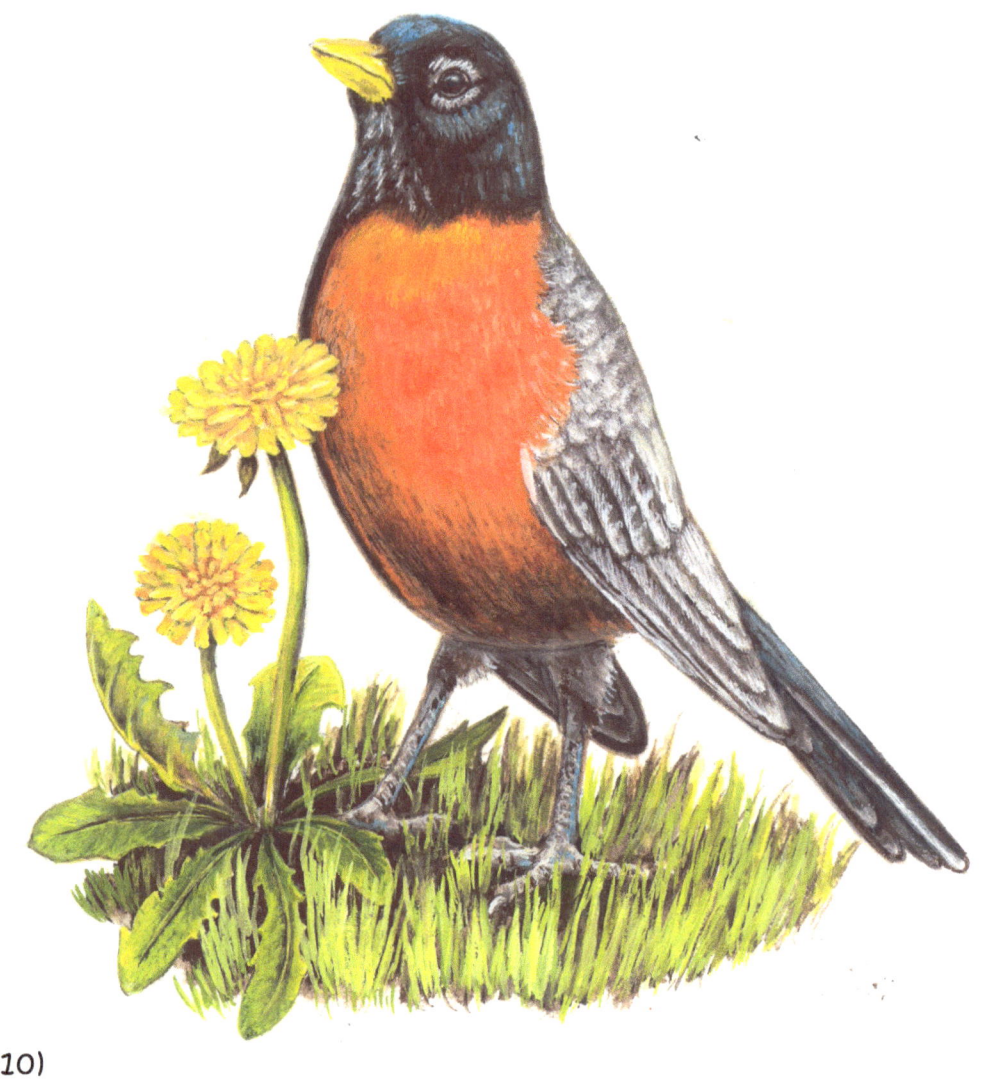

(10)

The last step! With a slightly damp brush, begin to blend the hard edges off the feathers. This part is a "back and forth" procedure. You'll have to add white, blend and then probably add more dark value. Keep adjusting your values until you're satisfied with the way the feathers, tail and upper legs look. On your last layer be especially careful to put some tiny strokes on the feathers going out to the outside edges to create some texture. Also, use White to paint in the streaks on the throat of the Robin.

Now, stand back and look at your painting. Make sure you've softened all the outside edges so the Robin doesn't look pasted on the paper. Check your values to make sure you have a full range from very light to very dark. Put the painting aside for several days and then go back to it and reassess.

Wood Duck
(Aix sponsa)

Colors Used: Permanent White, Burnt Umber, Ultramarine Blue,
Olive Green, Spectum Yellow, Burnt Sienna, Spectrum Red

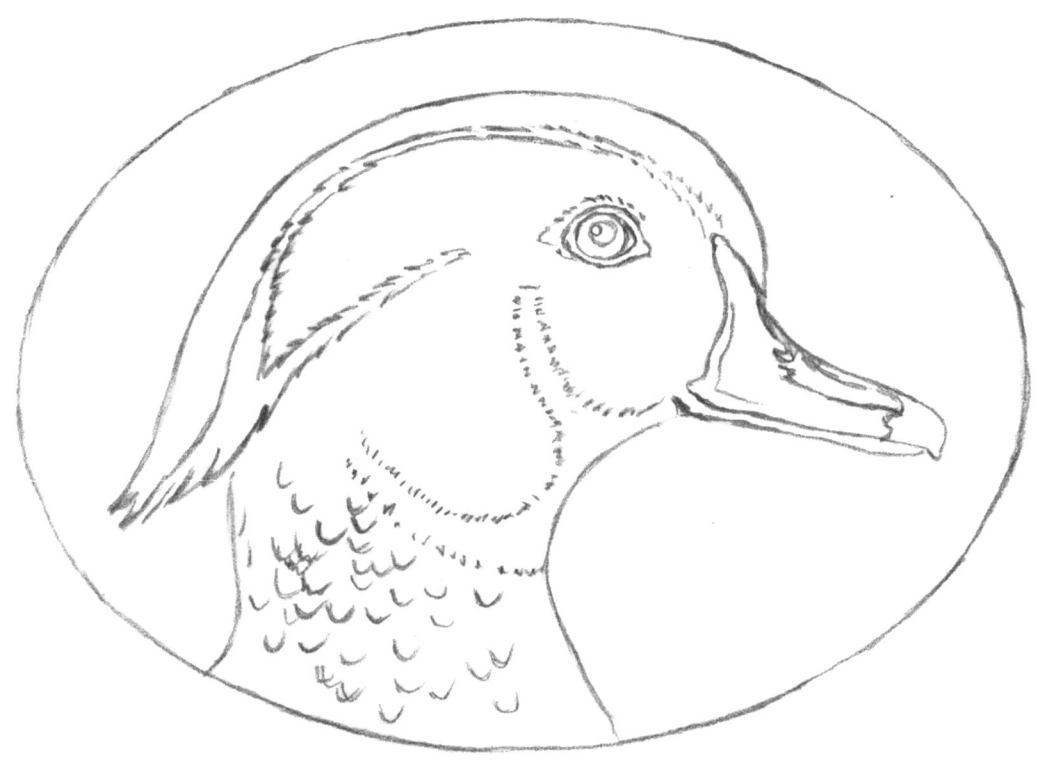

Use this sheet to transfer the image to your sheet of hot press
watercolor paper or illustration board.

Wood Duck Head

Colors Used: Permanent White, Ultramarine Blue, Burnt Umber, Olive Green, Spectrum Yellow, Burnt Sienna

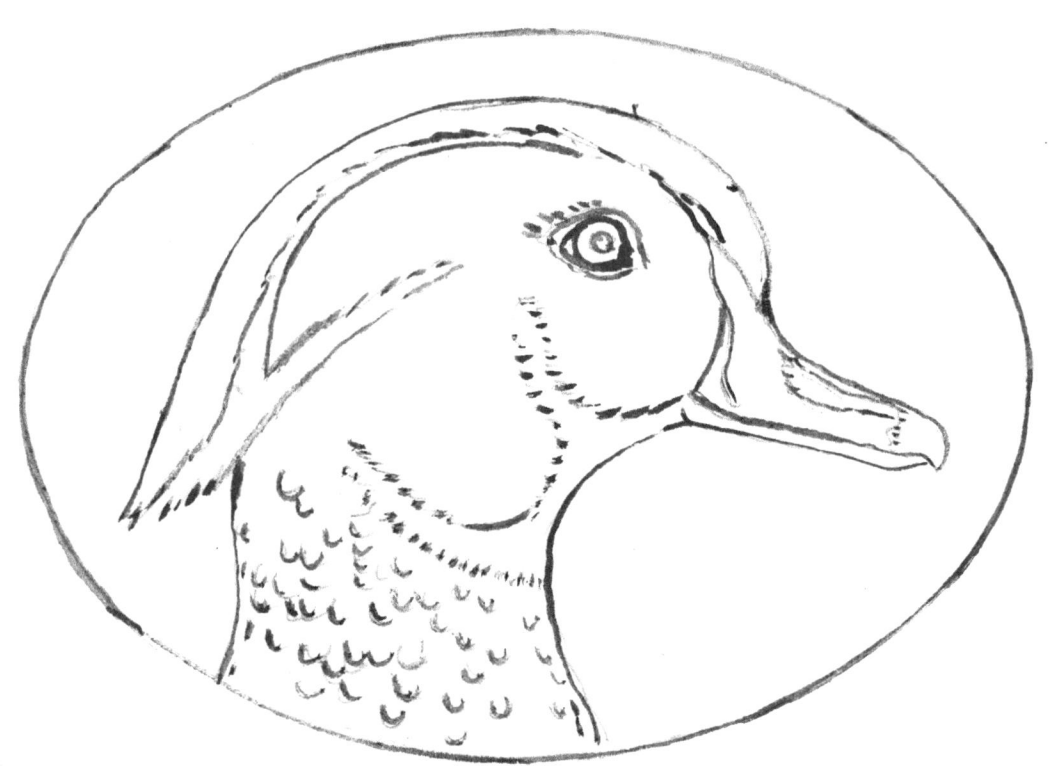

(1)

    Transfer your drawing to the watercolor paper (or
whatever substrate you've chosen). You'll be adding layers
of gouache so the lines have to be dark enough to hold up
while you're painting. I generally go over my lines with a
thin, dark value of gouache made by mixing Burnt Umber
and Ultramarine Blue. Keep your lines narrow. Use a thinner
wash than the one you'll use for the upper layers. Use one of your
smallest brushes. If your pencil lines are dark enough you
may want to skip this step.

Wood Duck Head

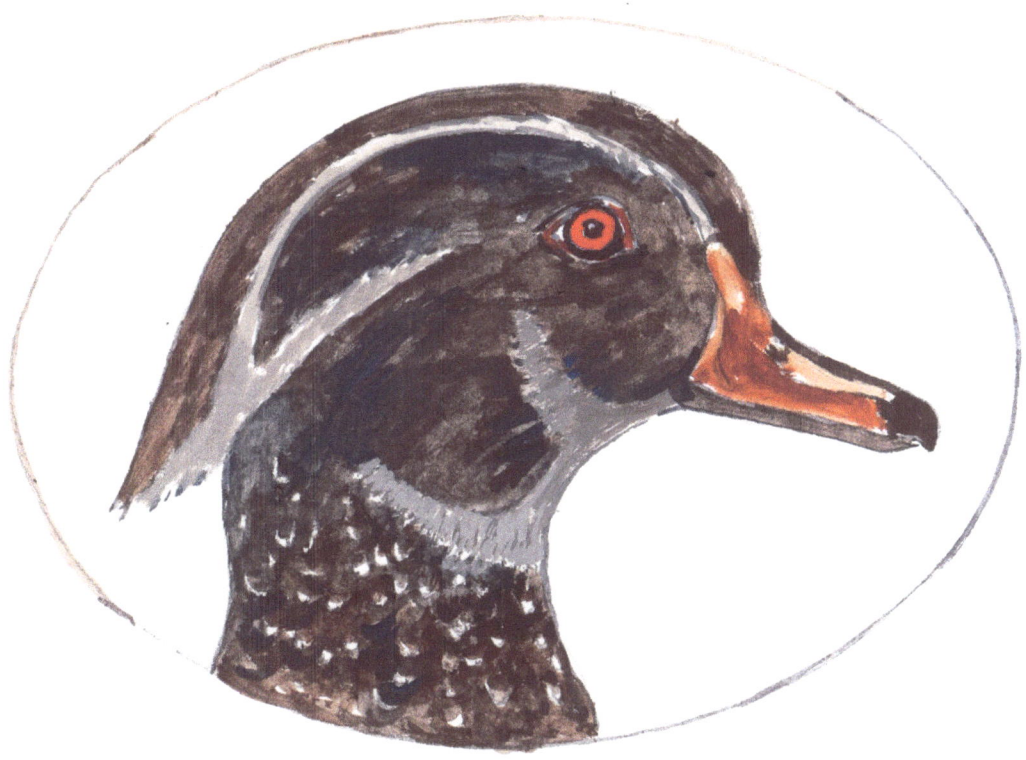

(2)

I won't be including a background in this demonstration but if you'd like
to put in a bit of sky, water or grass now is the time to do it before
you begin painting the duck.   Backgrounds are generally painted
first so that you don't have to repaint all of your edges later.
The Wood Duck will be painted with several layers of gouache, the first
layer being darkest and more watery and then building to a medium
value and then, finally, a light value layer. The upper layers will be painted
with a paint having a creamy consistency. In the early stages the
painting will look way too dark but that's normal. Use a dark mixture of
Burnt Umber and Ultramarine Blue to paint most of the duck as shown
in the illustration. Add a little White to the mixture to make a dark
gray and paint all of the areas that will eventually be white. There is an
exception to the dark underpainting method. When your subject will
have areas of very bright colors, especially red, a dark underpainting will
sometimes dull the color. So plan ahead! In this case, don't paint
a dark underpainting on the eye. Just paint it Spectrum Red.

Dont worry about getting an even tone at this point. You
just want to cover up the white of the paper. Use Burnt Sienna
to paint the bill and encircling the eye. Add a lot of water to
the Burnt Sienna and paint where the bill will end up being
yellow.

Wood Duck Head

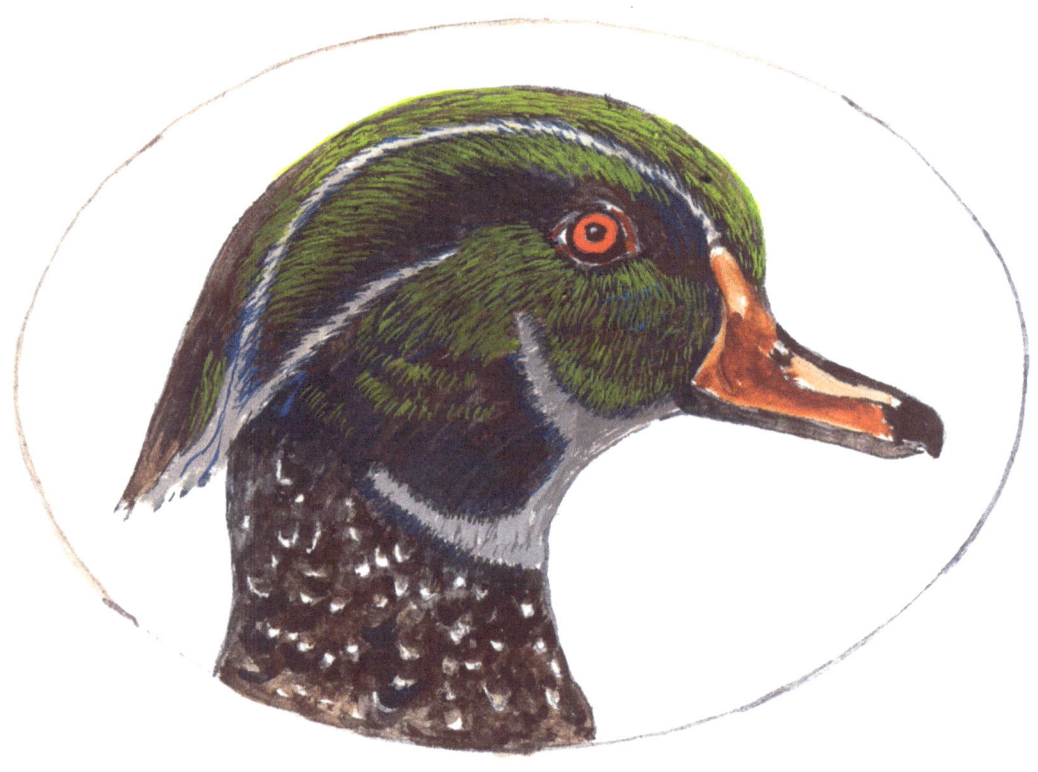

(3)

Use a Burnt Umber and Ultramarine Blue mixture to clean up the edges of the white stripes on the head. Use your smallest brush and paint short lines into the gray area that will end up being white.

Mix Olive Green and Spectrum Yellow, using more Yellow, to make a bright green of a creamy consistency. With your smallest brush, paint tiny lines going in the direction of the feather pattern. You don't want to make the strokes so close together that they completely cover the dark layer underneath. You want some of that layer to show through to give your painting depth.

Wood Duck Head

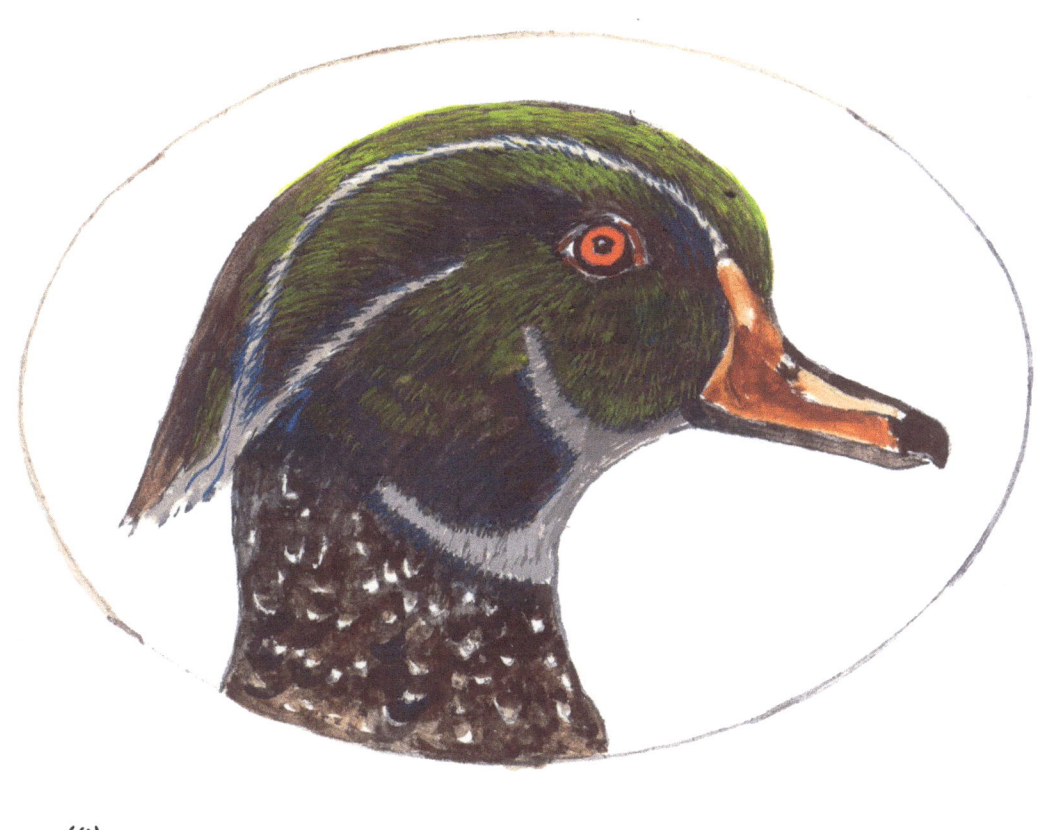

(4)

Blending has to be done cautiously. Its purpose is to take the hard edges off your tiny strokes but it's very easy to use too much water and blend too much which will wash away your underlying dark values. No problem. You can always go back in and redo your dark strokes with your dark mixture of Burnt Umber and Ultramarine Blue. To blend, dip your brush in water and then wipe it with a paper towel so that it's barely damp. Gently run the brush along your strokes, barely blending them in a little. This softness will give your painting a sense of realism. Blending will darken the value of your green layer but don't worry, you'll be adding another lighter layer.

Wood Duck Head

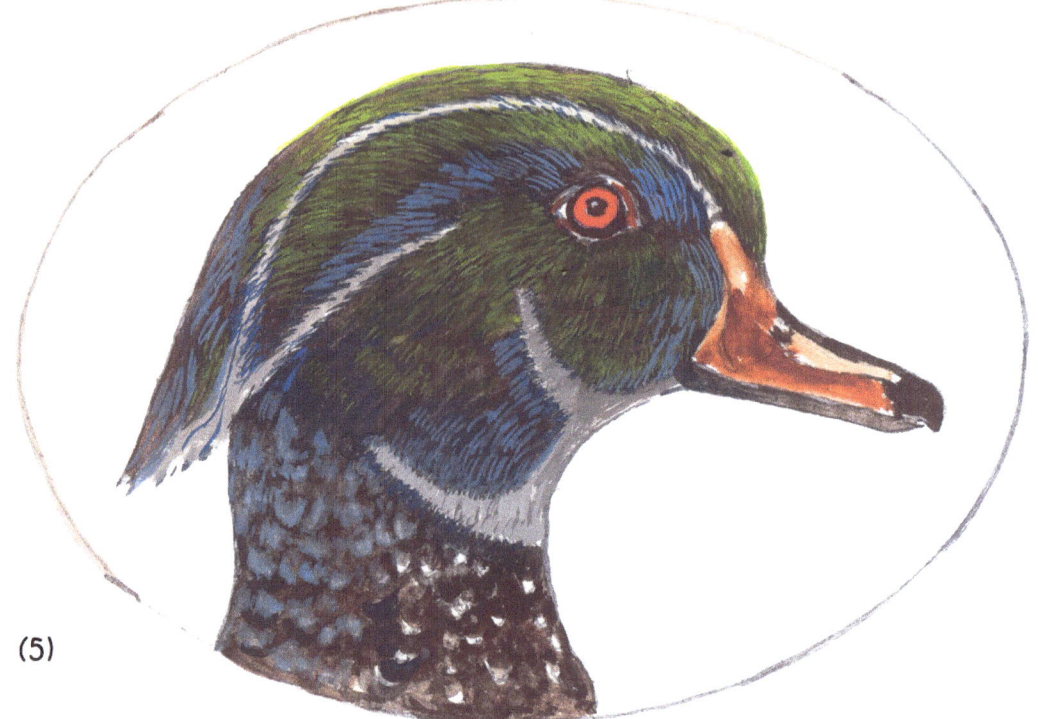

(5)

Add White to Ultramarine Blue to make a medium blue. Paint narrow strokes on the head and neck, always going in the direction of the feathers, as shown in the illustration. It might seem to be too bright but remember that you'll be blending your strokes and that will change the color.

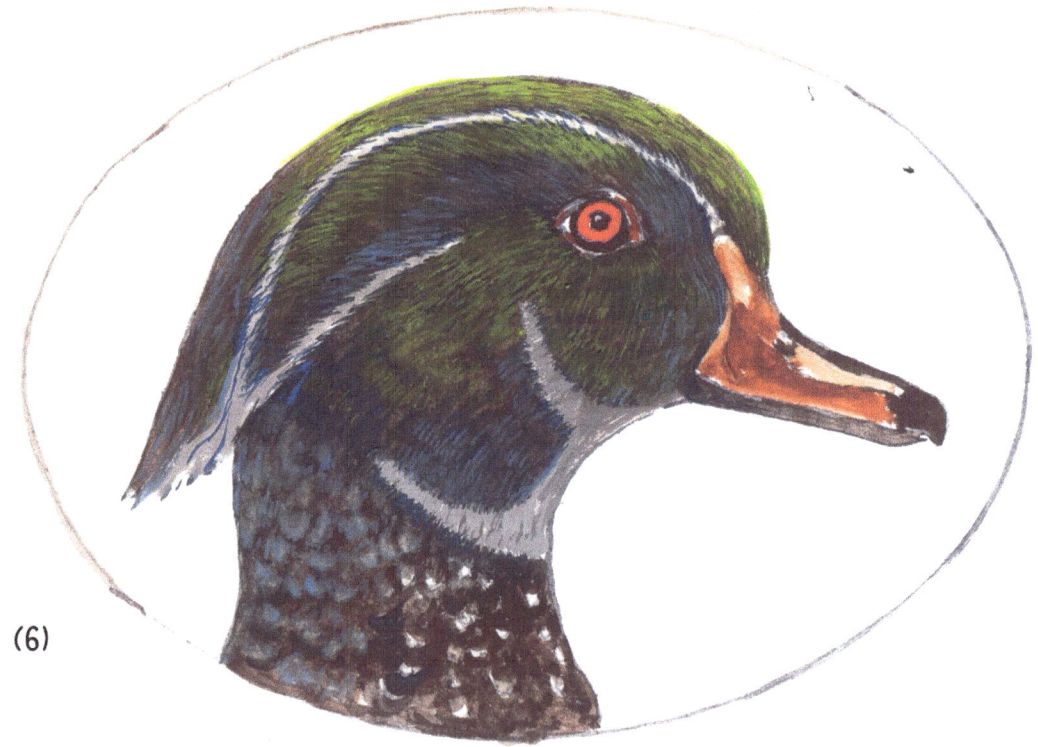

(6)

Gently blend the blue into the darker, lower layer so it can barely be seen. The blue should be very subtle. Your painting will still look too dark because you still have to paint the lighter values.

Wood Duck Head

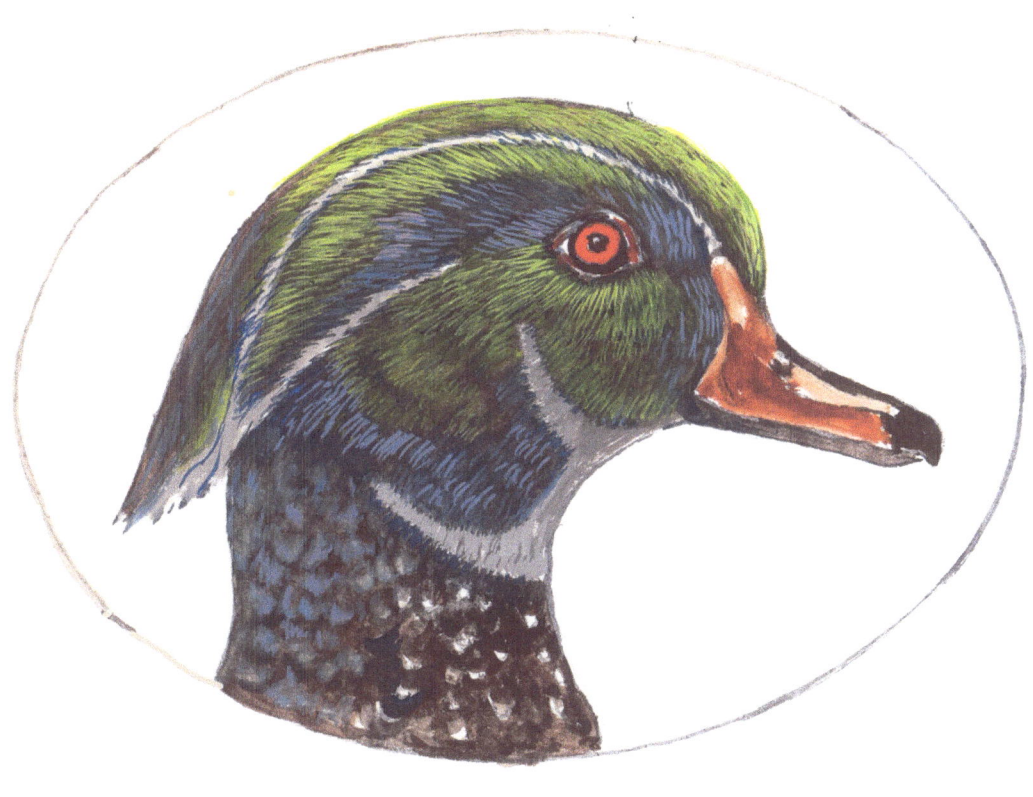

(7)

For the lightest values on the green areas of the head you'll need to add
a layer of Spectrum Yellow. Because this yellow is a little
transparent you'll need to mix it about half and half with white and
add just a tiny touch of Olive Green. With your smallest brush
paint tiny lines going in the direction of the feather pattern. It
might look a little too light at first but remember you'll be blending
a little and the darker color underneath will mix with it and make
it darker. With Ultramarine mixed with White and a touch of Spectrum Red,
paint short strokes over the darkest areas of the Wood Ducks head to
break up the areas of solid color.

Wood Duck Head

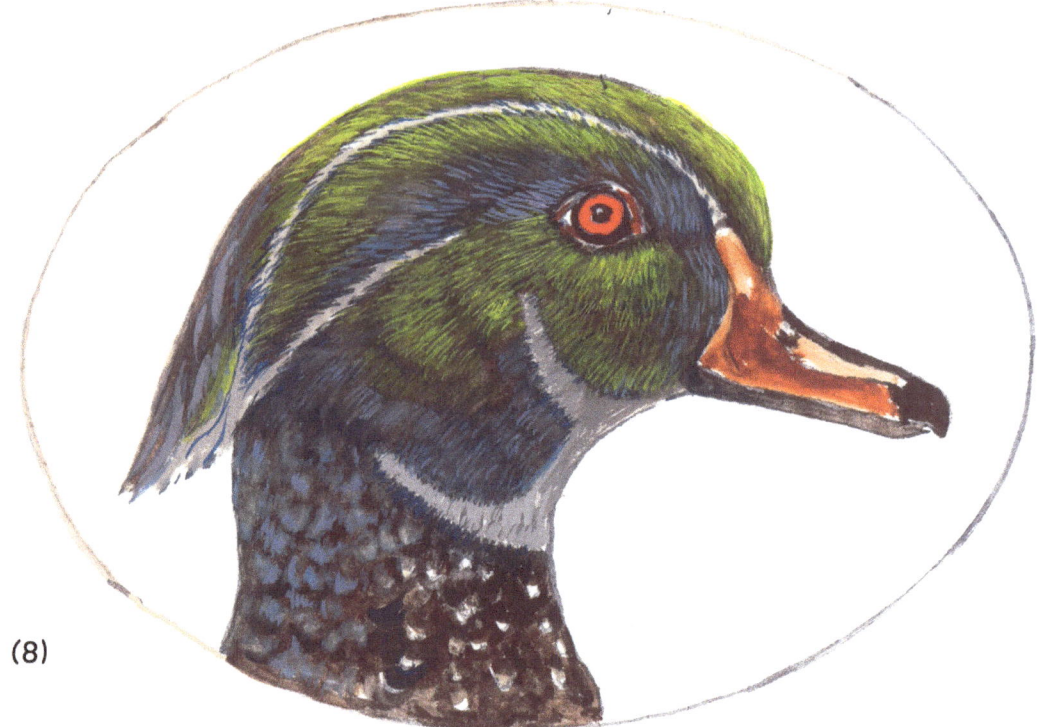

(8)

With a slightly damp brush, blend your strokes a little to soften them.
If you blend too much and lose too much of your darks restate
them. This is a back and forth process.

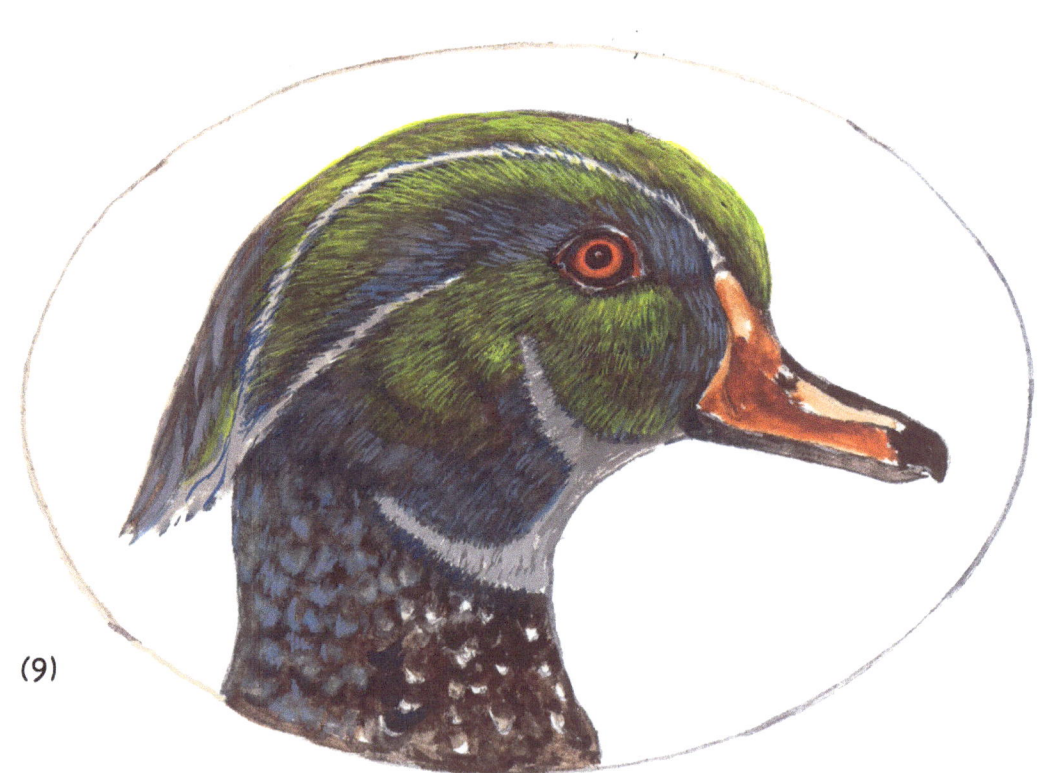

(9)

The Eye -- With Burnt Umber mixed with Ultramarine Blue paint the
dark circle around the eye and darken the pupil and make sure it's round.
Use Spectrum Red to even out the circle of the iris. Gently blend
where the red touches the dark of the iris.

Wood Duck Head

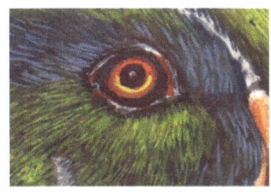

(10)

With Spectrum Yellow, paint a semicircle below the pupil.

.

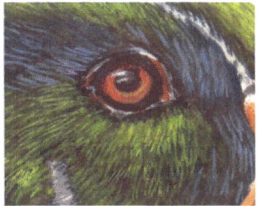

(11)

With a slightly damp brush, gently blend the yellow arc into the lower layer of red. Use Burnt Umber to paint a shadow on the top portion of the iris. Blend gently. With White paint the highlight in the pupil. With a tiny brush, soften the edges of the highlight. You may have to add a little more white to make the highlight pop.

.
.

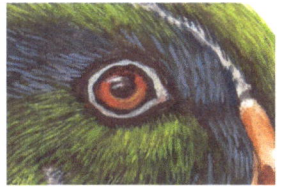

(12)

There is a yellow hue encircling the eye. To make sure the color is intense enough you'll need to first paint the area white.

.

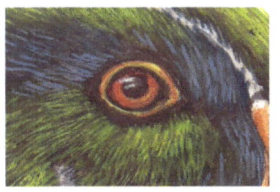

(13)

Paint Spectrum Yellow over the White of the ring. Add Spectrum Red to the Spectrul Yellow and paint around the outside edge of the ring. Gently blend away the hard edges. Then add white to Spectrum Yellow and add some highlights to the rim. Blend them in a little.

.

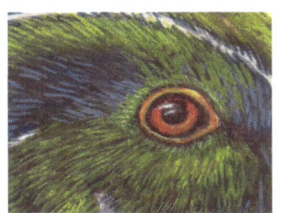

(14)

With a mixture of Olive Green, Spectrum Yellow and White, add the fine feather lines around the rim of the eye and gently blend and soften your strokes.

.

Wood Duck Head

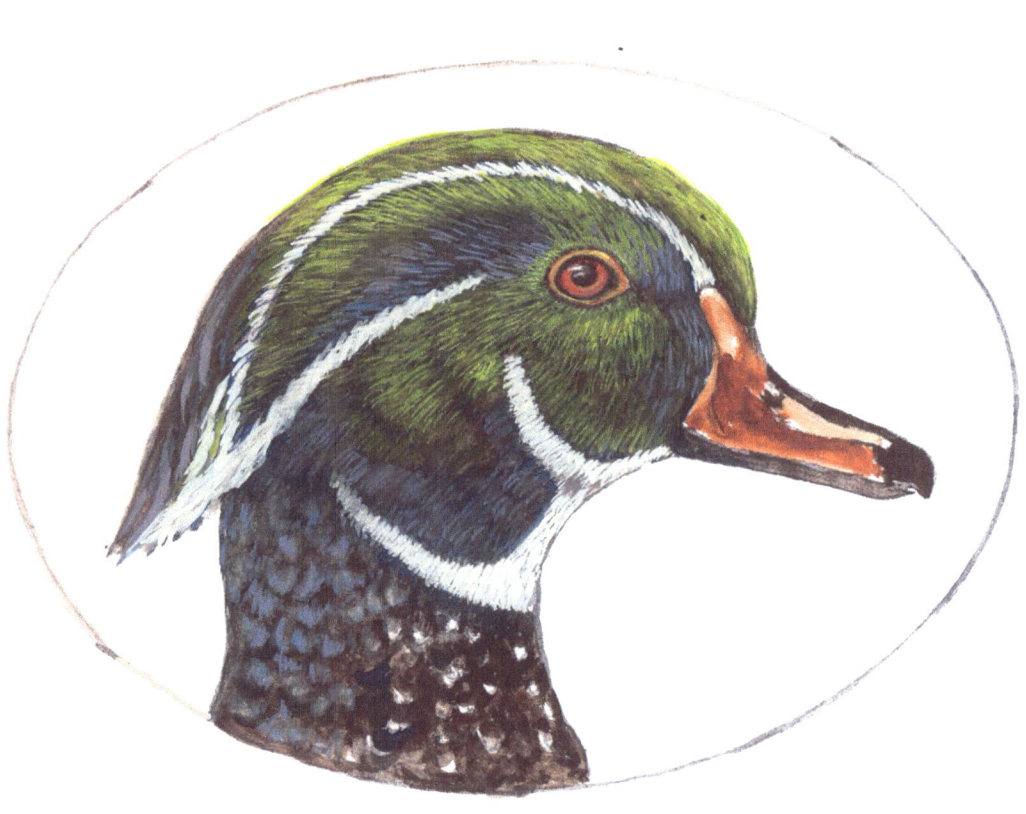

(15)

With pure White, paint in the stripes on the head and neck using very tiny strokes in the direction of the feathers. Don't worry about it seeming to be too white in places. When you start to blend the color underneath will blend with the white and make a variation in tone.

Wood Duck Head

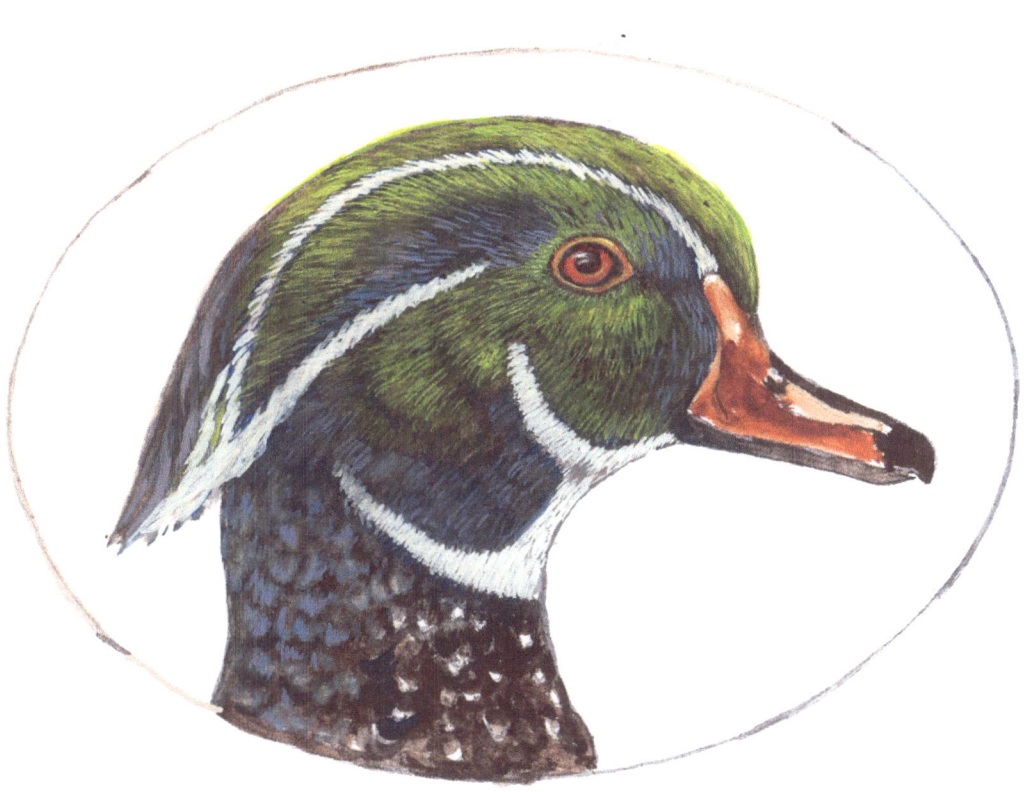

(16)

With a damp brush, gently blend and soften your strokes. The white will turn a subtle, soft gray. With pure White, restate the lightest areas. With your smallest brush, make your strokes in the direction of the feathers. Blend a tiny bit, leaving some areas white for impact.

Wood Duck Head

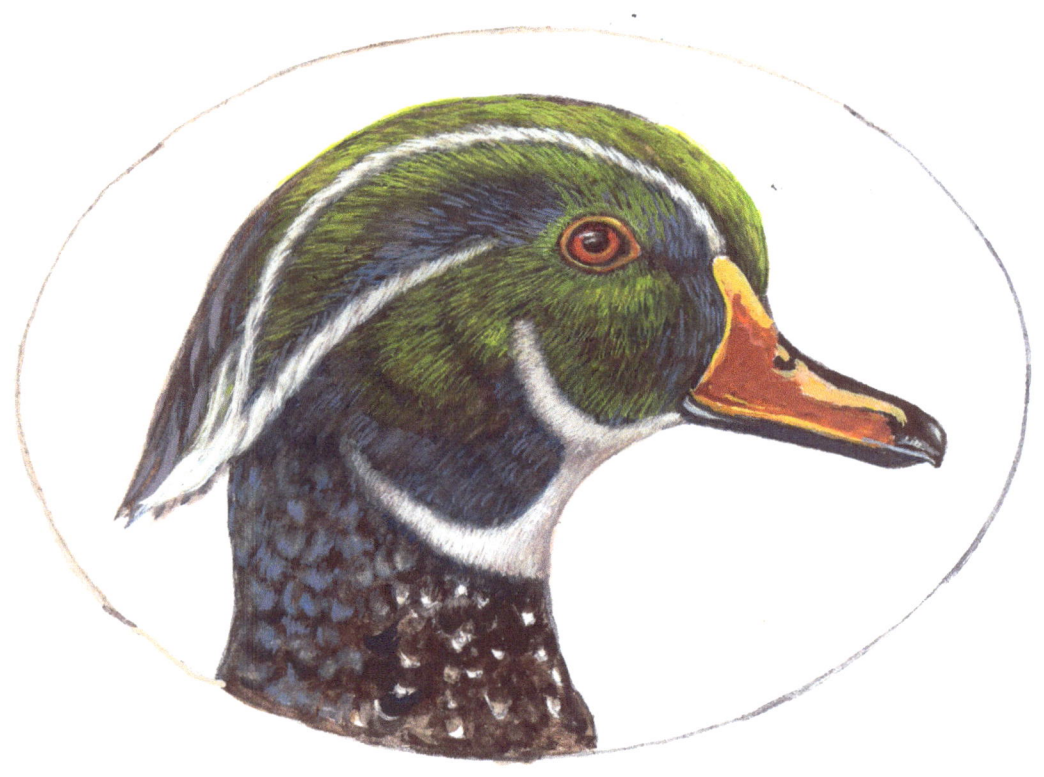

(17)

The Bill -- With a dark mixure of Burnt Umber and Ultramarine Blue,
carefully paint in the lower bill. Using White with a touch of
Ultramarine Blue paint in the little highlight at the inside corner
of the mouth. Use the same dark mixture to paint along
the tip of the bill. Also, use Ultramarine Blue mixed with
White to make the highlights on the tip. Use Spectrum Yellow
mixed with White to shape the yellow parts of the bill.
The white will make the mixture opaque and it will cover the
uneven areas. Use a mixture of Burnt Sienna, Spectrum Red
and Spectrum Yellow to paint the dark orange section
of the bill.

Wood Duck Head

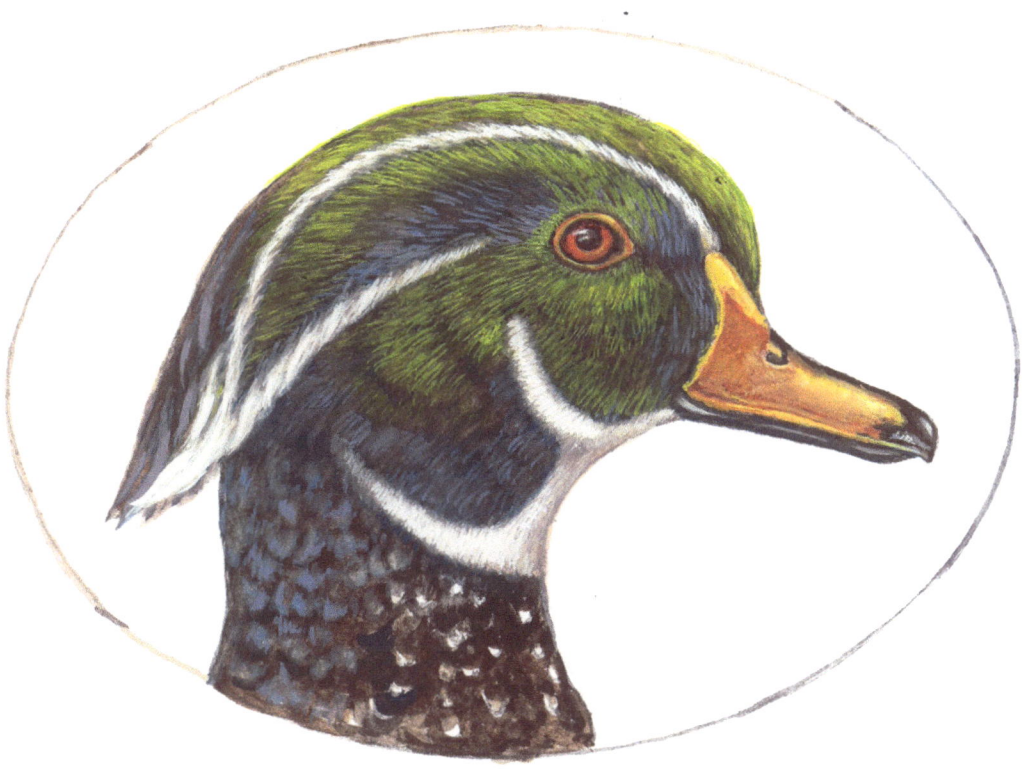

(18)

The Bill continued -- Begin blending the edges of the
different areas of color together. You will probably have
to add more color as you blend and soften the edges.
This is a "back and forth" process. Stand back from
time to time and check your values (lights and darks).
I added a couple more highlights along the side of
the lower section of the bill with Ultramarine Blue
and White. Especially don't forget to soften the edges
where the bill joins the head of the Wood Duck so it
doesn't look pasted on.

Wood Duck Head

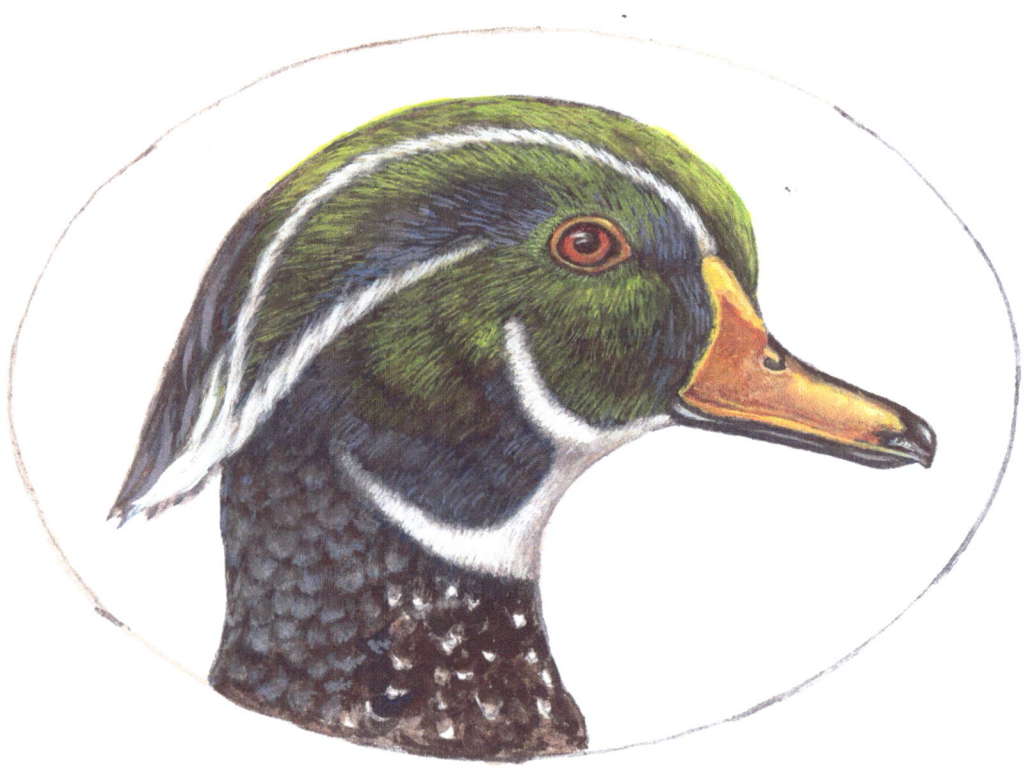

(19)

The Neck -- The back of the neck is in shadow so the color
is muted. The feathers have a bluish tone made
by mixing Ultramarine Blue and White. They're separated by
your darkest value of Burnt Umber and Ultramarine Blue. Make
your brush strokes go in the direction of the feathers and
the bottom of each feather should be rounded. The top
portion of each feather should be blended into the dark
tone of the layer below it.

Wood Duck Head

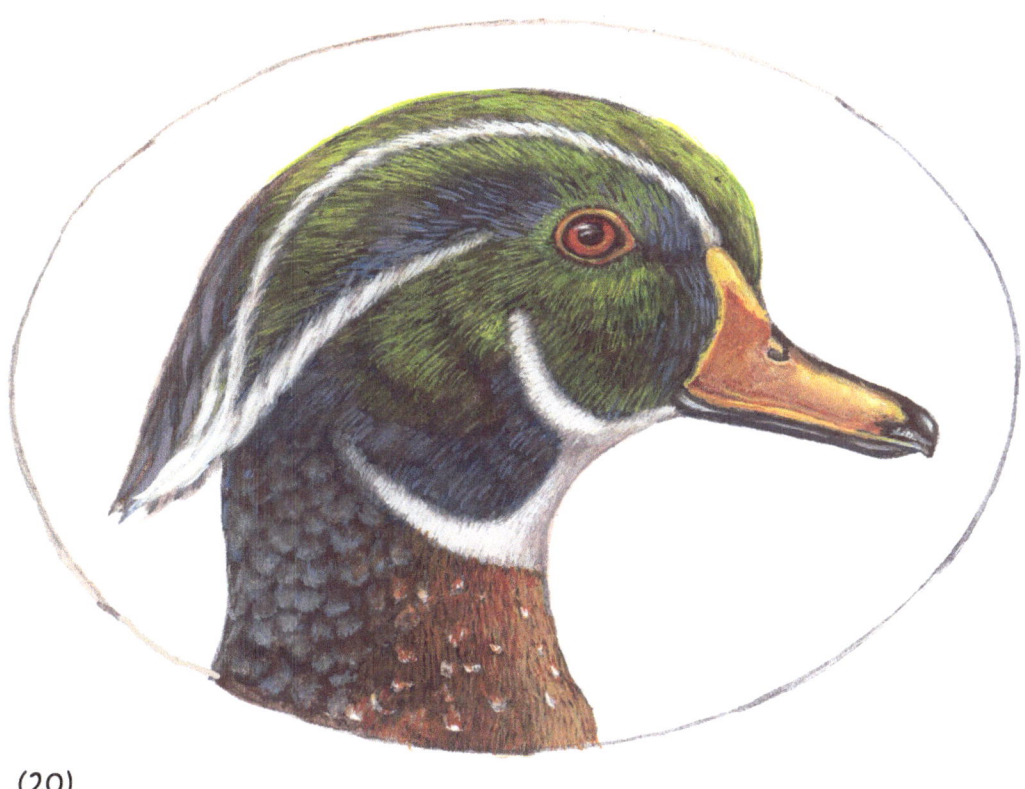

(20)

The Front of the Neck -- With a mixture of Spectrum Yellow
and Burnt Sienna, paint short strokes on the front of the
duck's chest. Add a bit more Spectrum Yellow
with the tiniest bit of White to the mixture and and paint
short strokes to highlight the very front of the chest.
Gently blend to soften your strokes.

Wood Duck Head

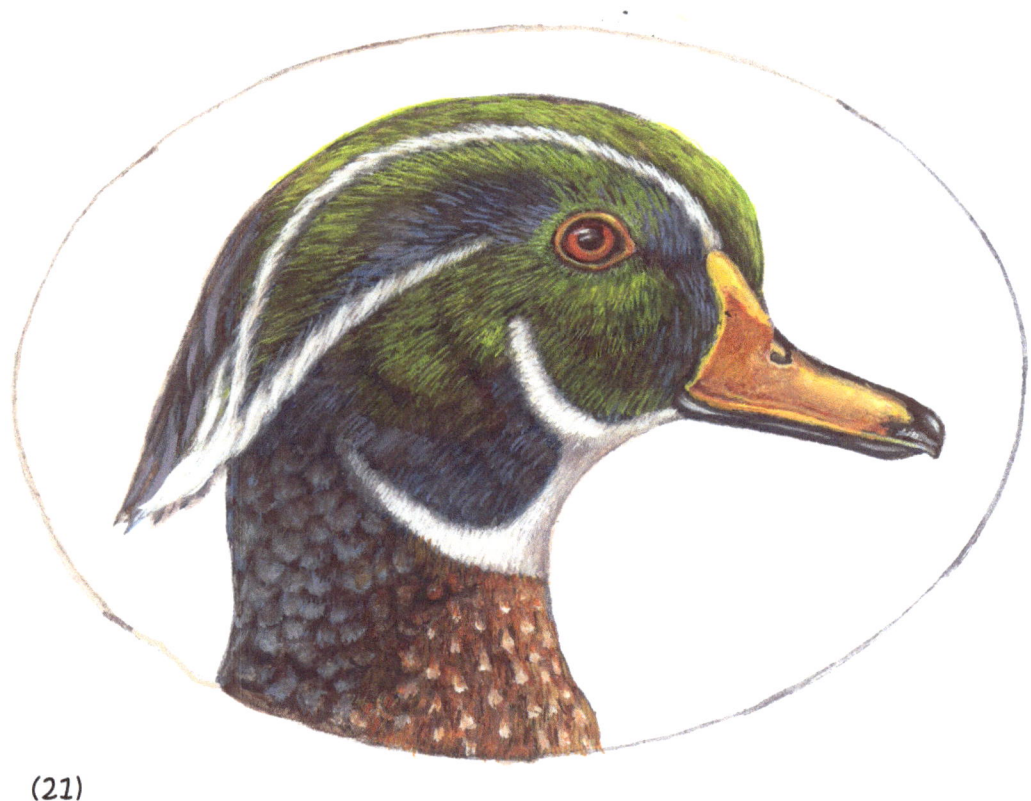

(21)

With pure White, paint small triangle shapes on the chest with the point of the triangles pointing upward. Blend the top point of the triangle into the sienna base color.

Wood Duck Head

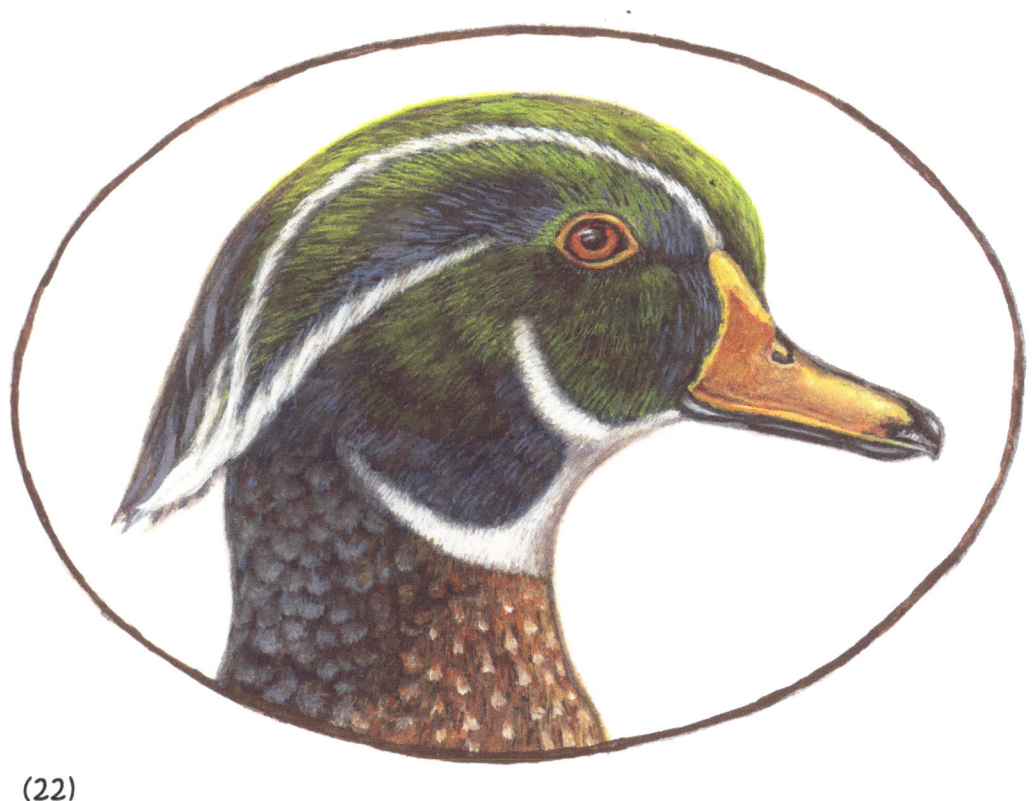

(22)

Now stand back and assess your painting. Check for values and how the overall work "reads."
When I compared my painting to the Wood Ducks in my many reference photos it seemed to me that the eye didn't stand out enough. I decided to darken the area below the eye and make the rim of the eye lighter. Also, it's very important to remember to soften all the outside edges of the Wood Duck's head so it won't look pasted on the paper. Sometimes I do this as I go along but in this demo I've saved it until the end and I've gently softened all the outside edges with a slightly damp brush all at one time.
I've also used Burnt Umber to thicken the oval encircling the duck's head.

It's always a good idea to put your painting away for a few days and go back to it later with fresh eyes. It will be easier to see where values and color adjustments need to be made.

Wrapping Things Up!

The same techniques you've learned to paint birds
in gouache can be used to paint so many of
the creatures and flowers we find around us.
Experiment and find out exactly what works
for you and what subjects most inspire you.

Most of all -- keep painting!

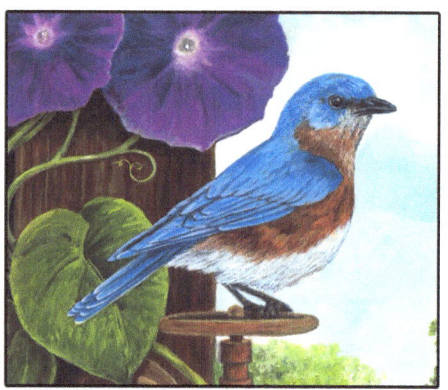

Thanks!

Sandy

Sandy

Please check back at
Sound of Wings Studio,
www.soundofwings.com,
for upcoming courses in
painting in gouache.

Other courses that are currently available are:
    Botanical Illustration in Gouache
    Botanical Illustration in Gouache -- the Four Seasons
    Painting Birds in Gouache
    Painting Animals in Gouache
    Painting Toads and Turtles in Gouache
    Painting Butterflies & Moths in Gouache
    Painting Garden Animals in Gouache
    Composing a Natural Science Illustration

And if you have any questions or comments
e mail me at sandy@soundofwings.com
I'd love to hear from you!

42